Lecherous, Licentious, Lascivious Lyrics

BY JOHN MILTON HAGEN

L-L-L Lyrics (Erskine Caldwell introduction)

Verse

The Shrewd Nude (A. S. Barnes)
I AM in Iambics

Anthology

Western College Songs (Robbins)

Plays

The Radio Murder Mystery
with Dana Rush (Longmans, Green; produced in New York)
The Band Box Follies, Daly's Theatre, New York
The Rah! Rah! Rajah, prize Stanford University play
Two off-Broadway plays

Original Song Collections
U.S.A.

Singin' in the Saddle (Boston Music Co.)
Songs of the Gold Miners (Carl Fischer)
Songs of San Francisco (Remick Music Corp.)
Bad Man Songs of the Wild & Woolly West (Sam Fox)
Songs of the Saddle (Sam Fox)
Ukulelepops (With F. Henri Klickmann, W. J. Smith)
Songs of the Roundup (With F. Henri Klickmann, Robbins Music Corp.)
Railroad Songs of Yesterday & Today (With Harry K. McClintock, Shapiro-Bernstein & Co.)

Great Britain & Canada

American Cowboy Songs (Francis, Day & Hunter, London)
Sherwin's Saddle Songs (Francis, Day & Hunter, London)
American Cowboy Songs (Canadian Music Sales, Toronto)

Lecherous, Licentious, Lascivious Lyrics

Is NOT the Title of This Book*

By JOHN MILTON HAGEN (ASCAP)

Foreword by Erskine Caldwell

South Brunswick and New York: A. S. Barnes and Company
London: Thomas Yoseloff Ltd

* THE VIOLENT VIOLET IS THE ACTUAL TITLE.

Library of Congress Catalogue Card Number: 69-14879

A. S. Barnes and Co., Inc.
Cranbury, New Jersey 08512

Thomas Yoseloff Ltd
108 New Bond Street
London W. 1, England

SBN
498-06912-5
Printed in the United States of America

Foreword

THE WORLD is in dire need of verse and verses the way John Milton Hagen does it and them.

Of course, maybe the world is a little bit behind times and is not aware of what it does need, but when the book "L" gets around, a lot of people are going to be brought up to date.

ERSKINE CALDWELL

Rheem Valley,
California

Contents

Lecherous,
Licentious,
Lascivious Lyrics

1

L-L-L-Lyrics Is Not the Title

AN EXPLANATION

"Lecherous, Licentious, Lascivious Lyrics
  Is not the Title."
But in these days of sexual hysterics
  Title is vital!

THE VIOLENT VIOLET

I would indite a triolet
About a violent violet,
But the violet's a gentle one,
So my fun is done ere it's begun!

TZIEGELE PHARTZT IN KRIEGELE

(Old Dutch Lullaby Adapted)

Tziegele, tziegele
  Vas phartzt in kriegele,
Bist hübsher als tziegele
  Vas phartzt in viegele!

BE TIDY OR WEAR A DIDEY!

Piddle, oh poodle, oh piddle no more,
Don't piddle in the middle of my carpeted floor!
If needs you must piddle a puddle, hear me:
Piddle on hive of hornet or bee!

QUOTH THE PREACHER:

I deny the pagan spittle
That each day we die a little;
Rather know we near the portal
Through which we're reborn, immortal!

WOMEN ANONYMOUS

(For Melony and Patricia)

All hail Anonymous Women of Letters,
Unsung throughout the ages!
(The typist is she whose initials you see
At bottoms of dictated pages.)

FRANTIC SEMANTIC

No recent news flash made me squirm
More than this'n:
"The man was freed *after a life term*
In Fed'ral pris'n!"

ILL PENSEROSO

(From the Hindu)

I loathe thee, lowly little flea,
Thou nippy, snippy frolicker!
Especially when thou grippest me
On my tender, gender bhallicker!

CIVIL WHITES

A demi-wit gave us this clue
  Regarding Civil Rights:
"All colored folk resent their hue
  And blame it on the Whites!"

ACTUAL, FACTUAL NEWS NOTE:

Skip worldly woe! Be still and know
  Before your art'ries harden,
The present Sheriff of Nottingham
  Just gave Robin Hood a pardon!

PACIFIST WITH A FIST

In Korea, Laos, Viet Nam (what next?)
  Our flags for "peace" are unfurled;
With this policy, will our folly see
  Us "pacifying" the world?

OH, BROTHER!

She had a dad incestuous,
  So she became a mother,
It proved, egad! tempestuous,
  For she bore him her brother!

LASCIVIOUS LASS

Gloria Victoria
Gloried in euphoria
  (No dreamy phantasmagoria!)
So, Gloria Victoria,
Though born in Peoria,
  Slept her way to the Waldorf-Astoria!

WILD & WOOLLY WEST

The Wild and Woolly West today
Still is-tenfold—twenty!—
They're wild about all western films
And woollen mills are plenty!

BIG OF BIG BUSINESS

A bus line's recent earnings, gains
Must have made it nervous:
In a flash it made a slash
In rates? Ah, nay—the service!

MODERN DRESS SEXPOSURE

If she must poach, encroach his job,
She will repel and vex him.
So to be sure of her allure,
She'll flex her sex to hex him!

ADD: HORRIBLE

Pups and kittens as advertised
Are ever described as "Adorable!"
But there must be some who are plumb dumb,
Anemic or mangy or horrible!

PUPLIFT UPLIFT

At last my pretty pup's a dog—
He's learned to lift on tree or log.
But, zest for uplift is most horrid
As he sniffs a female, season'ly torrid!

THE LEGAL BARROOM
(For A.B.)

My lawyer heard from a friend in the South
  This verse so terse and riant:
"Better a cat with a mouse in his mouth
  Than an attorney with hands on a client!"

RAINED CATS & DOGS

"You women all are cats!"
  He barked in accents grim.
"And all you men are dogs!"
  She meowed right back at him.

EMULATION OF A ROMAN DECLINE-NATION

Miscegenation
Is not on vacation

Once more incest
Is now sin fest.

Morality
Moved to a new locality.

Mosaic tablets
Now prosaic drug tablets.

Is a New Sodom and Gomorrah
Coming tomorrah?

SMILED WITH CHILD?

"The Mona Lisa Smiled," we read
  "Because she is to have a child."
"The Mona Lisa smiled," 'twas said,—
  Her doctor proved the rumor wild!"

NUDE BRAILLE?

Our attitude is not the prudest,
So we sympathize for a sightless Nudist.

BOTTOMS UP!

(For B.N.)

Delinquents are spanked in public in France:
Crime rate bursts like a bubble,
So why not chance a warmth to the pants
Of our American seat of the trouble?

POOR VERSE ON THE PERVERSE

I took my dog
On a lively jog
O'er crag and bog,
—Nothing

Ran him through fen
And thickest glen
Time and again,
—Nothing

Then raced him back
With leash held slack
To my humble shack,
—Nothing

And when I swore
I'd walk no more,
Then at my door
—EV'RYTHING!

AND NO PLOT BY GUM!

Movies ever lured the masses,
  But today it takes less doing:
Just produce whate'er surpasses
  Candy, popcorn and gum-chewing!

SHE CHANTEY

Why crave the wallop
Of a sexy trollop
When a lass of virtue
Can equally hurt you?

LET'S FACE IT

"Sure, they kin mate out of their race!"
  Said Mountain Auntie Joan,
"But folks will say that they've lost face—
  Could wed none o' their own!"

WOMAN HAS BUTTONS

"Woman's work is never done."
Never done? It hasn't begun!
Automation's here to stay,
Buttons make her work all play!

BREACH OF PROMISE

"It's just as we expected!"
  Screech all the Doubting Thomases,
"See how the new-elected
  Breach all their campaign promises!"

TINKER TO CHANCE TO TUNE TINKER

(For P.H.)

Great Composer stole a theme
From folk songs with his pen,
Songwright stole the music theme–
Folks have it back again!

"IT COULDN'T HAPPEN TO U.S."

Is the autocracy of bureaucracy
Destroying our democracy?

Is labor's tow'ring autonomy
Devouring our economy?

Is sexual amorality
Sapping our vitality?

Is socialism's gaudy guises
Blacking out free enterprises?

Is hist'ry portending our glorious nation
With the ancients' annihilation?

THE CASE IS FACES & PLACES

(For B.M.)

She's only second
To the prettiest of faces,
She's the gal (I've reckoned)
Who laughs at right places!

BULLDOG & MOTHER

Old England set Ma India free,
A moral's there somewhere to see,
What irony, what tragic joke:
Now India starves and England's broke!

NO NUDE PRUDE?

She was the prudest of lasses,
This no one can deny
Because she only wore glasses
To cover the naked eye!

ADAM'S EXPRESS COMPANY

Old Adam might have been most glib
In joshing his dear Eve ad lib,
But it's bare fact and not a fib
That he, himself, could take a rib.

A ROSE IS A ROSSI

(To M.B.)

Put this on your mind's hurdi-gurdi:
The name, Joe Green, is Guiseppe Verdi!

PALE FACETIOUS

A thought that comes to mind:
"Good Indians" that we knew
Were *traitors* to *their* kind—
It's all in point of view!

PSALM OF THE SALMON CANNER

To their dismay, they found all gray
The salmon they bought from Japan,
But as canners able they stamped each label:
"IT WON'T TURN PINK IN THE CAN!"

LIBIDIOUS LIFE OF A LAVENDER LOZIER

Or the Sex Biog of an Antediluvian Auto

(For F.Y.)

MOSHER bought a lavender
LOZIER, though owing his grocer and, in those days, his
HOSIER. Now recently came this revealing
DISCLOSURE in a bank inspector's detailed, damning

DOSSIER: In the Nineties so gay, for a gay gal, did
MOSHER float a big loan on the lavender
LOZIER, with a thousand still due the First National of
CROZIER. Yesterday came delayed

FORECLOSURE on Mosher's old Lozier since the
EXPOSURE. . . . Now on Leering Lew's Used Car
ENCLOSURE, ten dollars will land you the lavender
LOZIER! Now sure as your name isn't (or is it?)

DOZIER, there's a moral for playboys in this tale of the
LOZIER: The thousands for sex spent by Mister
MOSHER were worth a mere ten—*so you better stay*
KOSHER!

SLASH BASH

Me afraid o' that there boy?
Man, you got bats in your attic!
Sure: he packs a razor, Max,
But mine is automatic!

ALCOHOLIC FOR EXAMPLE?

Dandy kicks there are
And merriere
Than Life's swift kicks by far—
In the derriere!

POTATO PUDDLER'S PLAINT

Quoth chefs: "If soup's too salty,
Add a tater thereto!"
But if *spud* soup's thus salt-faulty,
Then what in the heck do you do?

BATHROOM FIXTURE PIXTURE

Sang a plumber as he strummed
On his nasal catarrh:
"Show me your bathroom
And I'll tell you what you are!"

AC OR DC?

(For M.B.)

An incandescent lamp are you
In fragile, glass habiliment,
Like burning coal (perhaps your soul)
Is your ever-glowing filament.

HAIR! HAIR!

A swim-beach he-man he would be,
But he'd nary a hairy breast,
Yet most ingenious lad was he–
Put a hair-piece on his chest!

PAPER REPASTO

(For B.W.)

Pictures on packs of some TV dinners
Promise some succulent snacks;
After dining on some of the TV dinners,
Next time I'll eat the packs!

IDLE SHUDDER
(For A.B.)

If all our states revolt, perchance
Against state-right invasion,
Would lone D.C. take fighting stance,
Or UN meet the occasion?

PERMANENT GUEST

Beware of the barbiturate—
You may become habituate!

CANDID ABOUT YOUR CANDIDATE

In public office, it's my thought,
Are few of my selection:
It's the best press agent that is bought,
Who oft wins the election!

SHORT SPORT SNORT
(For D.W.)

"All the world loves a lover",
(An adage old of sorts.)
But listen, men, we'll bet ten yen,
The world loves more its sports!

CASHED IN CHIPS

A hearse drove down the avenue,
A Brink truck followed nigh,
"Who said you can't take it with you?"
Remarked a stander-by.

SNIPE GRIPE

Masochistic pressure groups,
Who snipe and gripe at others,
Find dim delight to turn their sight
On their sadistic brothers!

NO SELF-CONTAINED ESCORT

She does equal work, demands equal pay,
Life's war she equally faces,
But when alone she must bemoan:
"I'm not equal to the task to go places!"

LIKE A RUN ON THE BANK

RANKLES, of course, to have thick
ANKLES, and a sometime ill-
OMEN is a bloated
ABDOMEN. And
HALITOSIS may cause a
NEUROSIS, but far most
SHOCKING is a run on her
STOCKING!

HARROWING!

Today the girls are most aware
Of care of their rare, and lovely hair,
Yet we know one who is most careless,
But she's a bitch—a Mexican Hairless!

CONSCIOUSNESS ETERNAL

As crabs have shell drop-offs
With no loss of life's breath,
So man his body doffs
And knows no so-called death!

ONE MAN'S MEAT; ANOTHER MAN'S METRE

Our modern concessions to sexual license
Have general approbation.
"But", quoth a sage, "it makes me rage:
This generation of degeneration!"

DRAIN THAT COW!

Some unions scream for thicker *cream*
When boss's profits thrive,
But not a word from them is heard
For *milk,* when earnings dive!

TIMING THE TOPLESS

"This topless thing to me is fun!"
Your tot might say at age of one.
"To me," thinks he, " 'twas not obscene
Exposed the time I had to wean!"

ON LOATHING CLOTHING

CLOTHING,
I view, with baleful gaze and loathing!
Far wiser was our dizzy globe
When all that man wore was a robe
There was no more to the sartorial score—
No male Schiaparelli, Klein or Dior,

Yet mortals did not look too weird
In little more than a flowing beard!

But, ah! today what do we wear
So that we may stay far from bare:
Come, let us list just for a starter
Shoe (or slipper) sock and garter.
A pair of briefs and yes! by thunder!—
Two shirts, one topside, one down under,
And if there's fat that you must hurdle,
Add to the heap one stout male girdle!

And then, of course, you must don tie
(Although we often wonder why.)
And clasp for scarf and links for cuff,
And if that stuff were not enough,
You must wear trousers, too, of course.
(Now you feel like a harnessed horse!)
To add to your vast inventory,
Cov'ring you with cloth and glory:

You wear two coats, a vest, a hat
And yet you're no aristocrat!
On all this vanity I frown,
Much simpler was the ancient gown!
No tailors' shears in bygone ages
When robes or togas were the rages!
How I wish I'd my umbilicus
Snipped in the days of Job or Micah's!

L'envoi

Of course, there's not the slightest harm meant
In passing by the *female* garment,
For it will need some other media:
A hundred volume encyclopedia!

FLEE THE FLEA

Deem not the little man
As not at all your match:
The wee, malignant flea
Brings a giant down to scratch!

LESS FEMALE UNDRESS

As gals grow male-ish and compete
With men, one thing is sure:
You must confess their dress grows less
That their lure may endure.

MERCY FOR THE MERCILESS

"Rehabilitated Murderers Pardoned,"
Is a governor's newest dictum;
Now could kind fate but rehabilitate
Each murderer's poor victim!

CRACKING WISE

The crabby crustacean
Finds slight consolation
On land or in the deep sea,
And faces frustration
And little elation
If he's not what he's cracked up to be!

NUDES TO YOU?

(To G.R.L.)

Gypsy Rose Lee once said it in prose;
Now into rhyme I make it:
We've oft met those who wear much clothes,
Who look entirely naked.

VOWEL TROUBLE

Old MacDonald had a farm,
E,I,E,I,O.
And while he'd plenty of kine and fowls,
He lacked two vow'ls—did you know?

QUICK MISCHA, THE MILITIA!

We've troops in Viet Nam, Cuba, Korea
And elsewhere far away.
Who minds the store (just an idea!)
At Home Front, U.S.A.?

RED HOT

(For E.S.)

How the Reds must have burned
As soon as they learned
That the trip to the moon we won,
But they'll burn even more
Should they try to explore
With a firstling flight to the sun!

POLITICALISTHENICS

(For W.C.B.)

New social measures sound so good
Till when they're fully understood;
But when you stop to think—oh, brother!—
They're from one pocket to another!

NO GRATITUDE IN US

Could be a carping attitude in us,
But aren't most speeches platitudinous?

SUDS IN YOUR EYE!

You hear them scream so loud, and louder
About the joys of washing powder:

Use BIFF or BANG or DIRT-GO-GETTER–
Each brand proclaims that it is better.

Buy ZING or ZANG! (each is superior.)
Try BOOM or ZOOM! (none is inferior.)

But Housewife finds these names becloud her;
Says simply: *"Gimme a box of powder."*

"NONE O' YOUR BUSINESS!"

(For J.R.K.)

Old Uncle Sam is in the red,
His business is a loss,
But if you're prone to run your own,
He'll show you who is boss!

ASININE ASPERSION

Who never makes the wolf-men drool?
A gal rear-ended on a stool,
And one not quite dissimilar,
Her derriere entering a car.

DERIDE THEM COWBOY!

"Westerns" thrill us to the marrow
Be cowboy deft or daft,
But once remove his huge sombrero,
Oh, pray, what have you left?

DOWN IN EFFRONTERY!

The sit-down crew is an oddball brew,
Flout law at their own election,
But faced with jail, they're first to wail
For the same law's full protection!

LIKE IKE & MIKE

We vote an hombre out of office
'Cause he was such a devious one,
And to our chagrin, we then vote in
A carbon of the previous one!

THE BIRDAGE FOR 4-LETTER WORDAGE!

Why not misspell, "dir", "gud" and "luv"
(All writ in lettered thirds) –
Aside thus shove the stigma of
The base "four-letter words"?

MINISTER TO THE SINISTER

To those who suppose that God is dead:
Your godliness is dead instead!

FREED BY WEED FEED

(Hippie Hymn)

You were intoxicating,
You were my sacred creed,
I'm not exaggerating–
But that was ere the weed.

You were a blazing jewel,
A precious gem indeed!
Erotic, torrid fuel,
But that was ere the weed.

Ah, you were like a cocktail,
A stimulating need,
Wouldn't trade you for an Airedale,
But that was ere the weed.

You were a Song of Sirens,
Piped from a Pan-blown reed,
You were a poem of Byron's.
But that was ere the weed.

With you *welt shmertz* was briefer,
A soulmate, cellmate freed,
Now I smoke you in a reefer—
Thank Satan for the weed!

YOUR NOSE KNOWS—OR DOES IT?

"An elephant smells like perfume,"
A zoo man said of its aroma.
To me it's like the smell of doom
And makes me nestle in a coma!

BEWARE THE SNARE!

Beware of the tender trap, young chap,
It could mayhap prove but claptrap!

DON'T DISHONOR HIS HONOR!

(For H.H.)

"Contempt of court!" his honor cried,
So off to jail we go;
We broke no law, we hurt his pride
And somewhere bruised his ego!

SAD SYLVESTER THE MAD INVESTOR

Or The Plunker's Plaint

(For J.D. III)

The banks do well with lending money,
Executives get sky-high pay,
Some workers earn big bonus honey
And mortgage fees just are not hay!

But lo the hombre termed, "Investor,"
(A docile soul and scarcely brash)
May get a green stamp each semester
(He only built the plant with cash!)

STOP THE PRESS!

(For C.E.W.)

As long as we make treasury notes
(Cheap printing press dinero, that is)
Let's give huge gobs to those sans jobs,
For we can print it almost gratis!

Bank holdup dangers we can stem:
When robbers reach the teller's lattice,
Don't hail the jail! Hand them a bale,
For we can print it almost gratis!

All industry could strikeless be—
An ideal spot where no more spat is:
They want more pay? Fill them a dray,
For we can print it almost gratis!

Gold standard we left long ago
Even silver no more fat is,
So now let's face it!—Pulps replace it
And we can print it almost gratis!

Then at this rate we'll be a state,
Where Ev'ryman a plutocrat is,
Till one day—CRASH! And cash goes trash—
Meanwhile we'll print it almost gratis!

LOW DEAL FOR IDEAL

We strive for ethics, spirituality,
But jungle law is still finality!

COLLEGE EXPLOSION

Taxwise we acknowledge
  We'll go in hock,
But we may soon have a college
  On ev'ry block!

PUBLIC PRIVATE LIFE

(For J.V.)

Complex, forsooth, are actors' rôles:
  Their woes and joys and sins;
They know not when the curtain falls
  Or play of life begins.

IT'S A BUST, BUSTER

"Oh, Papa, why do girls today
  Their chests display so prominently?"
"They ape us men, my son, but then
  They point up sex predominantly!"

SOLECISM PRISM

"*Celebrated* Criminal",
  One newsman wrote; (sounds glorious!)
Quoth a purist of a jurist:
  "Who then is notorious?"

WE LIKE A BALALAIKA

(For B.J.)

"A balalaika," said Russky Red
With a grin,
"Is slav man's inhumanity
To man-do-lin."

SLEEK CRITIQUE

(For P.B.)

He saw an "East Lynne",
Deemed it the worst,
Wrote: "He without sin
Stone the cast first!"

VEGETABLE CLOWN

Mother Nature's hearty joke:
The horny, thorny artichoke.

RELATIVES ARE RELATIVE

Tho' his age be thirty, forty or
A youngish twenty-one,
Since time began, he's still "The Old Man"
To his big or little son.

MOPPER COMES A-CROPPER

(For Arthur and Louise)

Quoth British Coz: "What irks me most
About you Yanks, is how you boast,
And when you dine, let's say, on roast
(I've witnessed this from coast to coast),
You handmop gravy with your toast,
So I'll jolly well write your Emily Post!

MAX HAD A MAXIM, TOO

OTTO had a
MOTTO and the
MOTTO
OTTO had, was: never drive your
AUTO when you drink and hadn't
OUGHT TO!

JAPANESE NOTE ON ARMENIAN MENU

"Rack o' lamb" is no
"Lack o' ram!"

AMOUR IN ARMOR

Oh, see Miss Sow Bug beat retreat
And roll into a ball,
So, tho' she's frail, the panting male
Arrives no place at all!

OF CONSUMING INTEREST

A quite quaint jungle shop
We'd say,
Would be a cannibal
Cafe.

BLACK COFFEE & WHITE RATS

Two scientists discovered that
Caffeine won't sober up a rat,
Which doesn't prove a thing but that
You cannot sober up a rat!

AIRCAST SECRET OF SUCCESS

(For J.D.)

You'd breast the crest of the ether wave
  With many a rich commercial?
Be audacious, pugnacious, reluctantly gracious
  And pretend you're controversial!

DENTAL TRANSCENDENTALIST

(For W.E.B., D.D.S.)

"For dentists I've no dread," he said,
  "I do not deem them ruthless.
"But it is sad to frankly add
  That I am wholly toothless!"

Y IN L D PDQ?

(For R.W.C.)

Rapid transit, jets and hustle,
Speedways, feedways roar and hum;
What a waste of bustle muscle!
Whither and where are we rushing "from?"

CONNIPTION PRESCRIPTION

One pharmacist you'd like to throttle
  (But all you do is glower)
Is he who simply pours a bottle
  And makes you wait an hour!

PENNED PIGMENT

SKIN, of course, may be no
SIN, but is the
TINT, a
HINT of
WITHIN?

ART OF ART

(For W.E.C.)

The artist loves his art and yet
He honors those with means to buy:
The rich man loves his wealth and yet
On artists casts an envious eye!

NOTE: AN ACTUAL, FACTUAL QUOTE!

Famed scribe, asked why
He chose to ply
The pen, said: [*cute!*]
"Like a prostitute,
At first it was done
Just for fun,
But later, don't *scoff, it*
Was done just for profit!"

JOCKEY IS NO JOCKEY

Do you recall when
A long ways back
When jockeys broke records
Only at the track?

"QUOTE THE RAVEN", UNQUOTE!

Beneath a tree with eager jaw
Devouring Poe's old "Raven", I
Sat reading, when from out the sky
A black-bird flew and jeered me—"AW!"

And then he fliply munched a straw,
Morosely drew a deep breath in;
Said I: "Oh, why the doleful grin?"
Quoth he the plural of this—"CAW!"

He smirked (amused at what he saw?)
  Said I: "Pray why, Sir Bird, grin you?
  Do I present a clownish view?"
And vehemently he croaked—"NAW!"

Then suddenly cried I in awe:
  "Black-bird, mistook you were, I know
  For The Raven by great Poe!"
With a nod he fled with loud "HAW! HAW!"

BIRD CAGE FOR BIRDHEADS

"Asylum in the Soviet",
  Some seek, but it's not clear
Why they can't find that for their kind
  We've many asylums here!

CALIFORNIAN'S COMPLAINT

(For F.X.K.)

Unless this constant dig for tax
  Eventually relaxes,
We soon will boast from coast to coast
  That we're the State of Taxes!

GREEK HIPSTER

(For Les and Nan)

The swarthy lad from Trinidad,
  Whose rhythms shake your hips so,
Obtained his name from some fair dame—
  A Greek nymph called Calypso!

BOBO THE HOBO

Said Bobo the hobo: "I wancha to know, Bo,
Why it's road and camp for me:
I may be a bum, Chum, but I ain't so dumb, Chum—
I'm the only one tax-free!"

OBESTIAL!

Fat chance, if you do only *wish* you
Could drop that adipose tissue!

MIND & MATTER CHATTER

In mem'ry's storehouse do you find
This "learned" kind of schoolday chatter:
"What is matter? Never mind!"
"What is mind? It is no matter!"

WORLD SHAKING EVENT

Do you care who's Miss Universe?
We don't—hence this puny verse.

NO FAITH IN FEAR

Quoth a seer:
(Not a clown)
"Faith is fear
Upside down."

OH, SEE D.T.

"Man Finds a Mouse,"
So goes the news,
"In His Soft Drink"
And so he sues;

Hence, drunks should win
Much bigger dues,
Who see pink tigers
In their booze.

HATE TO LOVE YOU

"Love thy neighbor as thy self",
A maxim tried and true,
But Joe's an elf who hates *himself,*
So what is *he* to do?

VEGETABLE LEAVES OF ABSENCE

"Use Pop-Up"—watch your pea plants hop up!"
(The ad. read. Proved incredible!)
The leaves grew more than six feet, four—
But not a single edible!

BEAR IN SHEEP'S CLOTHING?

We wonder if uncivil Lefts,
Who stir up public fights,
Are *some* of same who now acclaim
The cause for civil Rights!

OLD TIMER'S OLD TIMES

(For S.O.B.)

It wasn't 'cuz you wuz brave an' plucky
That you could survive;
In our wild West you wuz plain lucky
Jes' to stay alive!

POLITICIANS' CREED, TREED

They clobber Big Steel, Du Pont, G-M,
(They're a balloting minority!)
They court Proletariat and hope to marry it,
(They're in love with a voting majority!)

HONEST!

You need be no Diogenes
To frown on modern progenies!

BEAUTY & THE BEAST

(For L.L.)

ROAR the bulldozers,
GORE deep the
EARTH, huffing and puffing for all their
WORTH! Slashing and crashing all trees in their
PATH (perspiring cat drivers in need of a
BATH). But the patient old world accepts it in
STRIDE, never complaining of
EARTHRICIDE. Mere man decries the bruise to his
LAND, but a soulless machine cannot
UNDERSTAND!

GAMBLIN' ON THE GREEN

(For R.A.C.)

HOW sweepstake buffs in this
ENTIRE LAND
NOW gambol the green in
IRELAND! If we did thus in
AMERICA, Mister Bluenose would blow
HYSTERICA!

HERO IS A NERO

"Observe the *darling little sparrow!*"
Goes an endearing term,
But he's an ogre—chills the marrow
Of ev'ry bug and worm!

WE WILD & WOOLLY WEST

In San Francisco

(For H.C.)

It's roundup time on Market street,
On Geary, buff'lo roam,
On Grant, behold!—they dig for gold,
And Bush is the Redskin's home.
—That's how San Francisco looks
When you read some eastern books!

MONKEY BUSINESS

Even in the realms
Of jungle obscenery
There are monkey-wenches
In the simian machinery!

AVENUE REVENUE

(For F.X.K.)

An erstwhile collector of eternal revenue
Said in effect: "Good people, good heaven, you
Now pay taxes taller than a Pyrenee!
It's confiscatory! May lead to tyranny!"

So long as he is mercenary,
Man is pursued by the pecuniary,
And we'll wager a thousand to seven, you
Never escape eternal revenue!

FOUR LETTER WORDS

Without music

(For A.L.)

Four-letter words are now the fashion
To express the mundane passion,
While yesterday's terms euphemistic
Are viewed as too unrealistic.
But should you query me, good brother:
One extreme's unreal as t'other!

DREAM WITHIN A DREAM

(For E.R.D.)

As we rise from nocturnal dreams,
We wonder with consistence,
Shall we some day wake from this fray—
This frightmare termed, "Existence?"

UNDICTIONARY, LIKE "FICTIONARY"

You may speak of an actress, a Jewess, benefactress
And even (facetious!) an egress,
But there's resentment and most discontentment
On the non-Webster word-term of "Negress!"

FUN VS. DUN

(For R.W.K.)

Your class re-union once was gay,
Your fun unzipped like rockets;
Today fund-raisers hold full sway
As they unzip your pockets!

STEM TO STERN

Faking muscles, aft and fore:
Falsies today, bustles of yore!

COLT'S LOVE SONG

How I e'er could esteem
That old lass o' mine,
Today I deem
Horse's asinine!

OBSCENERY

Resent such words as lascivious, licentious . . . ?
Sue us for smut or libel?
We're not contentious, pretentious, sententious—
They're all smug-snug in the Bible!

BUNDLES FROM HEAVEN AND WELFARE

All hail the Welfare Agency
As we explode and populate!
They pay you a hefty *wage an' see*
You're thus inspired to propagate.

TYPE GRIPE

(For A.J.)

A newsman's headline read like this:
"THERAPIST CURES ESCAPIST",
But he went scarlet when he saw that varlet,
The Printer, spaced it, "THE RAPIST"!

BURP CHIRP

NIL is your
WILL to
SQUELCH a
BELCH!

NOT MINE BUT THINE

(For E.R.D.)

We pray and plead with Deity
  That *our* will He fulfill;
Instinctive spontaneity
  Tells us there's but *His* will!

GAMBLER'S GRUNT

Hark not to this smug goo:
  "Lott'ries are immoral!"
Insurance is a lott'ry, too,
  And there goes your moral quarrel!

FAIRY PRINCE MADE HER FAIRLY WINCE

The Black Prince would wed Fair Snow White;
Said he: "My child would climb in might."
Said she: "Your plea to me is vain—
Precisely what would *my* child gain?"

NON-CON?

(Moral for Delinquents)

Huber MacGoober O'Rangtang De Zormist
Boasts that he's a non-conformist;
But he's no wonder boy of the centuries,
For, non-conformists fill our penitentiaries.

PEDANTIC SEMANTIC

"A primrose," vows a wight who knows,
"Is but Miss Nomer for Miss Rose."

WORD TO THE WIVES

Gals, don't remake that man of yours,
Tho' he may need a trimmin',
For in the change his eye may range
To other lovely women!

DEAR ABBIE:

It's not that I am too much caring,
but why does many a maestro's bearing
suggest a near-sneer-leer he's wearing
or else wolfed down a kippered herring?

HOW SOME COMMERCIALS *STRIKE* US

(For P.S.)

ROAR it out!
POUR it out!
BELT it out!
PELT it out! Be
REPETITIOUS!
GET THE POOR FISHES!
ZOOM it,
HERSCHEL!
BOOM the
COMMERCIAL!

PIG IRONY

Quoth Married Bach'lor, "I confess
My life with Wife made a hog o' me.
And in the vernacula' I'm woise than Dracula
And 'step out' to relieve the monogamy!"

CHIC SALE COMMERCIAL

When dining near TV
You wish you
Could squelch that belch
On silken tissue!

PLAYBOY IN WORK

Let's drink and eat
And make Mary today,
For tomorrow, dear Mary
May be far away!

QUATRAIN QUIBBLE

"Will you step into my parlor?"
Said the spider to the fly.
"My zipper will not let me out,"
Came panting his reply.

VALID PALLID BALLAD?

I fled the leafless city soil
For the green scene of the country,
Where now bulldozers boil and roil,
Leave in their wake not *one tree*!

TRIBAL TONAL TAKEOVER

(For L.W.G.)

INTEGRATION hasn't reached its
GOAL? What of the blatant
EXALTATION of Rock an'
ROLL?

POX COMICA

Hang by your toe from rafter!
(It elicits screaming laughter.)
Swing like an ape from ceiling!
(It sends the audience reeling.)
Or, coyly drop your britches!
(It leaves them all in stitches!)
What's happened to the comic?
Bombed by the Age Atomic?

NO NUMBER, PLEASE!

These phony digits give me fidgets,
  I cry into my chalice:
As a man of letters I don't want digits,
  Or I'll take to digitalis!

CAN'T LEGISLATE LOVE

(For M. and B.B.)

Without hesitation
You can pass legislation
To press integration
Upon a nation.

But on reflection:
No votes or election
Can *force* your affection
In any direction!

SHED A TEAR FOR ONIONS!

(For Margot)

SILLY, but
WILLY NILLY, the
  ONION is a sort of
  BUNION, or ugly duckling of the family
LILY!

SUDDEN CORNY REVELATION

(For Maureen)

When you buy green corn on the cob,
(This is a scoop for the journals!)
You're getting chiefly a gob of cob,
But scarcely any kernels!

MOSES' NOSES

We knew a gentle gentile who
Loved not the sons of Moses;
It made him swear 'cause few now wear
The ancient tribal noses!

NOSTRUM ROSTRUM

Take Snoozo for good slumber,
Rowzo to stay awake,
Liquids without number
If urgent thirsts you'd slake!

Use Slizeoff if you're weighty,
Buljo if you're thin,
Peelit for face slatey,
Whoosh for pimply skin!

Pills for all ills earthy
To make you physically whole,
Drugs for the body worthy—
Rarely stuff for the soul!

2-B OR NOT II BE

"There are several ways of spelling 'tu,'"
But how to write this puzzles you,

Hence, why not try out something new
As "Scv'ral ways of spelling
'To'
'Two'
'Too'
'II'
'2'
'1 + 1'."

WHY TRY, CRY I?

(For T.F.)

"Experimental" Theatre Groups
Experiment with this and that,
Will someone tell pray what in hell
The're all experimenting "at?"

21 (GREAT) GUNS

The world was defied by the young king of Jordan,
Who sounded as tho' he was full of Gordon,
Though his talk and squawk seemed loud and Hunnish,
Recall when you were twenty-one-ish?

TO A JANUARY BELLE

(To M.S.M.)

They named thee Maybelle,
Belle of May,
Thou'rt lovely as
A summer day;
What paradox,
Then, greater than
Thou shouldst be born
The Twelfth of *Jan.?*

FOR THE LOVE OF KYOODLE!

"Oh, 'love me, love my dog!' " obese
  Miss Plumkin coyly sighed;
"I ain't no hog—I'll take the dog!"
  The bumpkin clown replied.

2

Prosaic Poesy

INTERPLANETARY SNOOPERS WE

Good gracious!—must we be rapacious and rend the nightie off Venus Aphrodite? Let sleeping maidens lie, quoth I, 'neath downy veils high in the sky!

HAMBURGERS FOR THE GOOSE,
CHOW MEIN FOR THE GANDER

If war broke out in Mexico, and China landed border rookies (with, say, a million bombs or so)—how would we like them fortune cookies?

R.I.P. THE COMMERCIALS!

Within our socialistic sharing, there's now demand for equal airing. If trucksters, hucksters have been slighted, injustice must be quickly righted. If singers, leftists and right-wingers have been hurt by aircast stingers; if robbers, dealers and free-wheelers have suffered wrongs, provide air healers! *(Eventually, Madames and Monsors, there'll be no room for broadcast sponsors!)*

THE POWER HOUR

(For J.R.)

They roar of power—black and white, 'most ev'ry hour, day and night. But we'll confess we rather stress the pow'r of the press—in *black and white!*

POLITICIAN WITH A MISSION

He vows he'll do his level best. Instead, stirs up a hornet's nest. And so—there's no need to pretend—he often gets stung—in the end!

FAREWELL WELFARE!

Newest taxes seem too great? Wish to escape such migraine fate? Just pull up stakes and emigrate to a Hate-the-welfare state!

3

Poetaster's Portraiture (fictional)

DRUGGED INDIVIDUALIST

(To A.T.)

They ranted of Freud and the New Analysis,
They panted on sex and the art of the phalluses,
They argued on atheism, Divinity,
Considered the morals of "outmoded" virginity.

They raved of wife-swapping and general depravity,
And all with the utmost of zest and of gravity;
Ofttimes the discourse found heights of ferocity
And seldom was marked by a shred of jocosity.

But never a word was heard from one member,
In their fiery gabfest he glowed not an ember,
So I asked him: "Sir, are you in anaesthesia?"
Quoth he: "No, I'm old-fashioned—stick to milk of
magnesia!"

LANGUAGE BURIER

"Of course not!" shrilled Savant de Zezbian,
"A Lebanese is not a Lesbian!"

DESPOTIC ANTIBIOTIC

The apothecary mercenary
Deserves to meet with "Harry Carey"
Or else at least a dose of flailing
For gouging indigent and ailing!

WHOZIZ FOR PRESIDENT

Our gramp's a champ at tiddle-de-winx—
Should be our president, methinks!

Chef Mori makes fine cacciatore—
An ideal leader of Old Glory!

Zoo-keeper Dunne is A-Number-One—
Should run the one in Washington!

You've guessed, of course, just what we mean:
Why should shrewd Hollywood steal the scene?

—AND GALLIC GARLIC!

(For N.K.L.)

"Boycott De Gaulle!", is the clarion call
Of people here and NATO's,
And so French dressing I eschew
And, too, French fried potatoes!

GRAIN BRAIN

I'll crown you Gheber of the Guzzle,
As sure as you are born,
If you can do a crossword puzzle
While full of Barleycorn!

RIOT AND RUE IT!

I decry unruly mobs,
  Their empty gabble-babble,
Yet the bloody ablution of the French Revolution
  Came from the unwashed rabble!

THE IMAGE SCRIMMAGE

So Lady Godiva rode nude on a horse
  To spite some masculine gender?
The truth was that she Took pre-L.S.D.
  And was off on an equine Big Bender!

Recall Napoleon's noble stance,
  How he stood as though bewich-ed?
Savants now decide 'Twas a nip-flea inside
  And Nap alone knew where it itch-ed!

Did Nero diddle-fiddle the while Rome burned?
  Wrote one who peeked into his windders:
"As a virtuoso He wasn't even so-so—
  He was merely brushing off the cinders!"

How did Mark Twain start his cigar-smoking chain?
  Why did he puff himself close to a coma?
When he met the miners, The bathless Forty-Niners,
  He thus quashed their piquant aroma!

Why did Washington stand while crossing that stream?
  Says our E.S.P. transmitter:
"It seems that he Was nudged by a bee
  Smack-dab on his Georgian sitter!"

Remember Mona Lisa's smile,
  So subtle, seductive, romancy?
But now we've found ground It wasn't profound—
  The artist just tickled her fancy!

TESTIMONIAL

"Will we have war forevermore?"
I asked old Colonel Estes;
Said he: "We always shall have war
As long as man wears testes!"

THE EYES HAVE IT

The eyes of light-blue crockery
Of love oft make a mockery,

And jet eyes can be treacherous,
Sea-green ones, methinks, lecherous.

Most grey orbs—intellectual,
And amber windows—sexual.

Some brown eyes sing of jollity
And violet globes—frivolity

But if you're in love's subjugation—
To hell with eyeball pigmentation!

NASAL FLORAL CHORAL

We rant of the scent of cyclamen
And many a fragrant flower,
But blench at the stench of a *flower* wench
(Like cauliflower gone sour!)

SLEUTH THE TRUTH FORSOOTH!

(For F.C.)

The lawyer hard degrees has earned,
But juries quash all he has learned.
The honest doctor must confess
His diagnosis could be guess.

Great science terms itself exact,
Then finds fictitious oft the "fact";
Philosophers do not agree,
Nor artists eye-to-eye can see.

So where is truth? In whisp'ing stars?
In robin's song? In gay guitars?
In crocus, rose or sweet verbena?
In love?—*Or far-off Pasadena?*

UNCLE U.S. ATLAS

(For L.H.)

In days of yore
The ancients swore
Old Atlas on his shoulders bore
The globe or more
From shore to shore—
Young Uncle Sam now has that chore.

TOT'S TERSE NURSE VERSE

How weird the sight of the "dead pan"
On the wee, wee mite on a bed pan!

SCHOOL O' THE BOOLA BOOLA

Phlegmatic, dour and acid tongue
And talent wan and frail,
To one big boast he ever clung:
"At least, I went to Yale!"

Positions many held he, still
Each one was doomed to fail,
Success in others made him ill—
At least *he* went to Yale!

Art critic, tailor, teacher, mime—
He trod a sorry trail,
Excoriating others' climb,
At least he went to *Yale*!

And on his stone with sculptor's pen
Was writ in letters pale:
"Where *goeth* he, we do not ken,
But we knoweth he *went* to Yale!"

INANITY OF VANITY

I would not dare offend
Your foible or your sin,
But where does stubbornness end
And will power begin?
Ah, it is clear to see
After a thought or two:
It's will power in me.
And stubbornness in you!

VIDEO CRITIC'S SOLILOQUY

As confided to us. The confidence betrayed thus:

Since TV critic's my employment,
I hope for video enjoyment;
And do I find it most rewarding?
You be the judge from this recording:

One star leapt in a tank of jelly;
A pregnant one discussed her belly,
While some indulged in cream-pie flinging,
A few like crows cawed—called it singing.

Two comics did some tragic throating,
A senator went self-promoting,
Some advertised (for free) their platters,
A group discussed some feckless matters.

Commercials, strident, broke in—many!
(I made a note I'd not buy any!)
And now they plan *pay* television!
They should pay me—that's my decision!

ANCIENT JEST UNBUTTONED

The foremost artists, too, have erred,
So grieve not when you feel unsainted—
Great Michelangelo, we've heard,
Old Adam with a navel painted!

1-MAN WAR ON WAR

"American offensive war
Should now be banned forevermore!
Examine most of our great strife!
What price the awesome loss of life!

"The Revolution won with gore
Yet, Canada is free sans war!
The fray betwixt the Blue and Gray
Might have been solved a peaceful way:

"We could have paid the loss of slaves
With cash, avoiding countless graves.
The Spanish-Cuban war, they say,
Was staged. (A newsman's holiday!)

"Horrific World Wars, we surmise,
We should have joined, but with supplies
Of ships and planes and gold and such,
Compared with life, a price not much!

"Our frightful Asiatic 'Cause'
Deserves but scantest of applause:
Are we police of all this sphere?
Sufficient problems have we here!

"All wisdom, mercy, truth have fled
We worship gold, hold cheap the dead!"
Thus spoke a sage, reflective man;
Let us gainsay him—*if we can!*

SICK COMEDIAN'S PLAINT (SIC!)

GRIPE have I at one
TRIPE-
COLUMNIST, who's dreary, dull and daft, the
SOLEMNEST! He dreams he teems with wit and
MIRTH, when he's but stuffed, unlaundered
SHIRT! He craves his paper's top
ACE SPOT—this scissor-man with fat
PASTE POT. In words of Groucho (or was it
SOCRATES), spare me from mealy-mouthed
MEDIOCRITIES!

L'ENVOI

On second thought I am
CONSTRAINED now to admit he's brilliantly-
BRAINED, and I regret all that I've
SAID! (Today he gave me a column
SPREAD!)

UPCHUCK MUCK

The slick "sick" comic
Makes us vomic!

PRIMROSE PATHOS

LAD:

Oh, prim and proper primrose free,
But still a lovely rose,
Come trip the primrose path with me
On twinkling, naked toes!

LASS:

Thy prim and proper primrose free,
Step-daughter to a rose,
Wilt walk the primrose path with thee—
Stout buskins 'round her toes!

LAD:

Oh, prim and proper primrose free
But still a lovely rose,
I'll walk the primrose path with thee—
With buskins thy sole clothes.

LASS:

Thy prim and proper primrose free
Will be thy walking rose,
But clad, dear lad, in chastity
Of thorns from head to toes!

FINIS

MONEY-LOOSE WOMAN

I call my wife a wanton,
But don't call me a rat;
I call her such because she's much
A-wantin' this an' that!

THE SOLOIST

Jasper MacCasper O'Walberg Von Blott
Was distant toward women, the kaboodle and lot.

For chastity he hadn't resolved,
He merely shuddered at becoming "involved."

And yet his libido demanded its due,
Which was a big something he couldn't eschew,

So a biblical wight he would emulate
(See Genesis nine in chapt. thirty-eight!)

Though of honies and bunnies he did *own a list*,
He solved the hard problem—he turned onanist!

MOCK THE SOC!

(For A to Z.)

Why do political mediocrities
Dream they're wise as Socrates?

PUPPYHOODWINK

You've heard of dogs of slight acumen,
Who deem themselves as wholly human?
Well, I've a pooch whose puppy noodle
Regards me as a fellow poodle!

POST HASTE: MOST WASTE!

(For F.N.K.)

Titus St. Vitus O'Beegum Du Champ,
To save the price of a postage stamp,
Drove his auto over dale and hill
Merely to pay his telephone bill.

Pincus MacDincus Gazincus Von Frost,
A bookkeeper friend, told Titus the cost
Of his journey to save a paltry few cents
By driving five miles in his Bercedes-Mentz:

"To save a mere stamp, your wear and tear,
Insurance and gas and stuff like that there,
Conservatively, your expense
Was forty-nine dollars and eighty-three cents!"

YOU'RE EVER ON STAGE

If you're a beauty or a wit,
You, too, must be a *rare actor*:
You cannot shirk, you're ever at work—
You must remain in *char-ac-ter!*

WEIRD BEARD

A midget visited a camp
Where bare life is a breeze,
Quoth he: "It's mysteree to me
Why they all wore goatees!"

TALE OF TWO CITIES

San Francisco Speaks:

We have a rugged splendor,
You look like a drugged bender,
We've fog of Hi Fi vintage,
You've smog of eye-cry squintage,
We've lots of fair-sex charmers,
You've acres of ex-farmers,
Your envy'll never irk us,
(We're drama—you're mere circus!)

Los Angeles Speaks:

'Frisco, you're too frisky!
You're loaded up with whisky!
So we ignore your vitriolics,
You high-proof alcoholics!

PARITY CHARITY

(For F.C.)

Some causes may orate, *"Donate!"*
But go deaf when you holler:
"Just what percent of our cash is spent
On those who need the dollar?"

BLEAT OF THE MAN IN THE STREET

Good teachers, yea, deserve more pay,
But I've this thought in mind:
Their twelve-month pay today ain't hay
For just a nine month grind!

TOP BANANA IN A TOPCOAT

(For Al Santos)

Should you in supermarkets stray
In topcoat with large pockets,
Just watch the clerks eye you with dirks,
Their orbs nigh out of sockets!

FLIGHT OF MONEY

ROCKETS' cost to reach the moon isn't
COMICAL! The cash from our tax
POCKETS aptly
ASTRONOMICAL!

AFRICANDID CAMERA

Despite our great elation,
Could self-determination
Upon examination
Prove self-extermination?

D'D IF YOU DO & INDEED IF YOU DON'T

Lubrishka MacGrowse—
  O'Jyna-De Blutch
Nagged her poor spouse
  For drinking too much,
So he took the dry pledge,
  Now she calls him most crass
'Cause now he will hedge
  At *one* social glass!

CHARITY GLOBULARITY

(For J.K.B.)

One day I sent five modest dollars
To a school for Zombi scholars,
And from this quite slight gesture noble
Soon resulted pleadings global:

Camps for dolphins, whales and sturgeons,
Halos for surviving virgins,
Plaintive pleas and frantic squeezes
For a fund for flea diseases.

Homes for stray and poor Venusians,
Cash to back Manx revolutions,
Overcoats for Riff and Zulu,
Lollypops for girls named Lulu.

As he staggers 'neath such mailing
For the "worthy" and the "ailing,"
Wretched postman is bent triple
May become a needy cripple.

While I'm not a welfare ducker,
I've been placed on Roster Sucker
All because I sent five dollars
For a school for Zombi scholars!

SECOND HAND INQUISITION

(For B. and N.W.)

A modern unreeler
Of The Inquisition
Is the used car dealer
On television!

NOT A DASTARD!

The poetaster,
Clearly,
Is merely
A poetic bastar'!

INTEGRATION CANINE

My dog, despite a pedigree,
Knows never social barrier,
So long as she's a she, this he
Forthwith is glad to marry her.

Come, learn a lesson from my dog—
We may find living merrier,
So let's prove wise and mongrelize—
(If you'd be hound or terrier!)

SLOB McPHOBB

Adelbert McPhobb
Was a goodnatured slob,
  But his humor was foolish and ghoulish;
What he laughed at most vastly
Was ghostly and ghastly—
  Pure corn right off the macabre!

LULLABY ADULT

Life is boresome
For a wife who snores some;
True, her spouse roars tympani—
But so does a symphony!

TV CRITIC (TO HIMSELF)

All beauty contestants look alike—
  The same snare smile,
  The same hair style,
All beauty contestants look alike.

All beauty contestants look alike—
  The same bone stance,
  The same stone glance,
All beauty contestants look alike.

All beauty contestants look alike—
  The same bra shape,
  Inviting rape,
All beauty contestants look alike.

All beauty judges look alike—
  The same sex play:
  "Does she say, 'nay'?"
All wolves (or judges) pant alike!

BORE SNORE BOOK

I bought a book on sleeplessness
And must confess it was a mess!—
So dull each page and paragraph,
I fell asleep in a minute'n half!

FOR CRYING OUT LOAD!

(For D.C.)

The bases all were loaded
And the faces which exploded
With cry and oath and boo,
Proved fans were loaded, too!

GOSSAMER GOSSIPER

"She has a Sunday face,
My deahs,
But she has Sat'day night
Ideas!"

HARD TO SWALLOW

(For A.G.)

New laws, blue laws, far from few laws
Rest uneasy in our palates;
Bold laws, old laws and untold laws,
Aimed for politicians' ballots!

PIN ON HIM A SYNONYM!

(For S.I.H.)

Our economics is for comics,
It's rife with clownish tricks.
To be precise, isn't "Fair Trade Price"
Monopolistic fix?

SEXANALYSIS CRITIQUE
(F.N.)

One Hector Goonflecktor Bullwinkle Dalrymple
Was a good stock broker, sure, pure and simple,
He mastered the lore of the trade, gains and losses
And soon became one of his firm's chief bosses.

His background, artistic and literary
Was mostly quite minus if not wholly nary,
But when he became a near-aged twilighter
He longed for the fame of a best-selling writer.

So, gifted with a tape-recording memory,
He ground out his childhood like sheer, human emery
And gave it the title of (quote) "Grammar Grader,"
A neat idea for a mundane stock trader.

Then, published by clients, his sharp business smeller
Soon made "Grammar Grader" a near topmost seller.
Another such fluke he never created,
But fame now was his, though somewhat belated.

He hired an expert in good self-promotion,
And courted the press and clubwomen's devotion,
Gave autograph parties and "aired" his knowledge
And taught writing hopefuls in high school and college.

But pride's like a bubble (see Ecclesiastes!)—
His fame was bombed by a nasty of nasties,
Who wrote of the book in brief criticism:
"A sharp self-portrait—literary onanism!"

MAN MAY MAKE THE CLOTHES
But Clothes Don't Make the Man

My body's but a suit of clothes,
 The Real Me is its wearer,
A suit of clothes can scarce know woes
 Or any human terror.

My body's but a suit of clothes,
  Without it I'm no barer,
A spirit elf is my true self,
  A thread-bare devil-may-carer.

HULA-LA LEI

(For B.P.)

Do ever view the graceful hands
Of dancers in Hawaiian lands!
But mainland male skips finger tips,
Is rivetted by hula hips!

MUNITIONLESS PLANET

"Venus must be peaceful," said
  The wag, "with all her charms."
I asked him why; he made reply:
  "Venus has no arms." (!!!)

THE SEE SHORE

"Let's have a beer bust and a swim!"
  Said he. Said she: "We must!"
It was no joke when her strap broke,
  But it proved one fine bust!

MADRIGAL OF MARRIAGE

When he was but a lad of twenty,
  And known as Handsome Harry,
He met young maids and old aplenty,
  All anxious for to marry.

And now since he is old and bent, he
  Is known as Hairless Harry,
And meets young maids and old aplenty,
  All anxious for to marry.

WINDMILL & BAG

There was a man who fought windmills,
  A Spaniard most neurotic—
As we recall, like one "The Gall,"
  Quite quaint and queer, quixotic!

INANITY OF VANITY

Ah, vanity of man
  And his petty, prim self,
Deems none bigger than
  His Mighty Himself!

Mayhap there may be,
  Unseen to the eye,
Greater mortals than he
  In earth, sea or sky?

THE ABSURD BLURRED WORD

(For M. and F.R.)

The botanist, quite learned, he
  Most sorely has me treed,
Declaring a eucalptus tree
  Is but a giant weed!

And cometh now the religionist,
  Yea, verily, non-caustic,
Who sayeth that an atheist
  Is but a shy agnostic!

And then there was the father, one
  Of ancient parenthood,
Who, whaling hell out of his son,
  Sobbed: "It's for your own good!"

We nearly missed the militarist,
The weird sort of fud-*duddy*,
While, jailing G.I.'s, will insist:
"It's protective cus-*tody*!"

Euphemistics and semantics,
And linguists and pedantics!

TAX BY THE PACKS

"It is no joke to smoke—you'll croak!"
Shout many good physicians;
"Puff stacks of packs, relax (for tax)!"
Spout pelf-eyed politicians.

UNMORAL TALE

He was a wanted crim'nal,
Who choired behind a hymnal,
And it was mighty shrewd o' him,
Disguised behind a pseudonym.

He hid foul deeds felonious
In manner sanctimonious,
Though moralists may hoot at him,
Oh, wasn't it quite cute o' him?

SMOKE AN ARTICHOKE!

Confess! (And we intend no joke)
But if you're folk who do not smoke,
Do you not find ash trays a mess?
Confess!

"Sure!" admit the folk who smoke,
"But we have viewed chewed artichoke
At your good house—like pure manure,
Sure!"

So we indite on our veranda
These cogent bits of memoranda
By way of social propaganda:
Apple-sauce for the goose is dross for the gandah!

SWEET RICH BUM

She told her chum: "My old, rich bum
Can double-date and treat us:
He's a double sugar-daddy now
Since he got diabetes!"

ROCKETEERS

(To M.V.)

The Russians built a rocket ship
(Then followed asininity!)
So we built one and they built one
And so on to infinity!

WHAT PRICE BARGAIN?

A kind of selling sign
On which trade seems to thrive:
Is "PRICE: JUST 99".
[Marked "down" from 65!]

??? AND !!!

When I make query curious,
My spouse goes tongue-penurious;
When naught I ask my spouse at all,
Her words splash like a waterfall!

CORRECTION!

Change the words and let us sing,
"Love is a many spendthrift thing!"

ALL SWEDES LOOK ALIKE
(To V.R.S.)

All Swedes look alike,
But so do the Dutch,
Hungarians, Bavarians—
The latter quite much!

All French look alike,
But so do the Gaels,
Roumanians, Ukrainians
And people of Wales!

All Asians look alike,
But so do the Greeks,
Alsatians, Croations,
And Mozambiques!

All folk look alike
As well they should—
Created, related
In one brotherhood!

PRESS AGENT FOR PRESIDENT!

In public office, it's my thought
Are few of my selection;
It's the best press agent they have bought
Who oft wins the election!

POLYGAMY IS BIG O' ME!

I fain would marry Mae,
But Mae's not fair as Beth;
I cannot marry Beth
Since she's not sweet as Fay.
But Fay's not good as Ann,
And Ann's not bright as Dot,
But I cannot marry Dot,
For she's not wise as Nan.

But Nan's not cute as Sue,
  And Sue's not chic as Jean,
But I cannot marry Jean
  Since she's not smart as Lou.
But Lou's not warm as Jill
  And Jill's not neat as Peg,
But I cannot marry Peg
  As she's not fine as Lil.

But Lil's not nice as Bess,
  And Bess rates next to Myrt,
But I cannot marry Myrt
  Since she's not dear as Tess.
I deem them all divine—
  Each one my queen I'd crown;
Polygamy might be big o' me—
  But they've all turned me down!

COLORED LOVE

My love has purple tresses
  And eyes of brilliant red,
My love wears ragged dresses
  And has a swollen head.

My love has lips of ebon,
  Her ears are lust'rous green,
She has a yellow web on
  Her ecru-colored mien.

My love has cheeks most shapeless,
  A glowing, bulbous nose,
I shudder, were she drapeless—
  What charms could *she* expose?

Why love I such a creature?
  How fell I in her net?
She's a color-t.v. "feature"
  And I can't adjust my set!

DECEMBER DITTY

If a body meet a body
  Comin' through the rye,
I hope each body had a toddy
  The cold spell to defy!

THE TAXPAYER'S LAMENT

—With Dulcimer, Sackbut & Shoehorn
(For L.S.)

Why am I toiling for Communist Tito,
  Sneering old Egypt and Turkey and Spain?
Why lose my pants to De Gaulleist France,
  Why did I buy them guns, goods and grain?

Why am I working for Germany, India,
  Nippon and South American land?
Why are my savings all whittled like shavings
  For steep local taxes I can't understand?

Why are my pockets ripped open for rockets
  Paying for whimsical flights to the moon,
Spending like crazy, supporting the lazy
  While my pulp dollar shrinks up like a prune?

Why am I keeping the United Nations,
  Why waging foreign wars with my pelf?
Yea! I am boiling to think I am toiling
  For all the damned world—excepting myself!

WELFARE STATES

They heighten and tighten the might in
  The Bureaucrat Titan!

BRAUMEISTER'S WATER CHOLER

Oh, where's the beer of yesteryear
  With zing and zip and zest?
Today most brew (is it not true?)
  Is brown H_2O at best!

POET'S PATHETIC PLEA

My pome don' rime,
Don't scan in line—
  Ripe cheese, and I should bury it!
So 'round my throat
Bind on a rope
  And make me Poet Lariat!

ANTICS OF SEMANTICS

(For V.G.)

Comes now the latest language scrimmage:
"We must maintain The Public Image!"
Will someone now inform us nicely:
The Image of just *what* precisely?

HEAVENS, YES!

Atheist's Air

The moralists urge us: "Be good
  Move in saint-like direction!"
Pray, would we not be bored a lot
  To live such sheer perfection?

BARNYARD BALLAD

Oh, see the hen strut while she's pickin',
  So proud of foot and leg-o!
A haughty bird, this off-spring chicken
  Of an inflated egg-o.

YOU'RE THE JUDGE!

Your doctor is skilled in medicine,
  Your banker knows his pelf;
Your lawyer his law, your dentist your jaw—
  But *judgment* rests with yourself!

Your realtor knows his realty,
  Your broker's a convincing "Delph,"
Your sainted minister knows good from the sinister—
  But *judgment* rests with yourself!

The architect plans your domicile,
  Your boss *thinks* you're for the shelf,
Your teacher may be a know-all creature—
  But *judgment* rests with yourself!

The judge deems himself omniscient,
  Your folks may have named you Yo*delph,*
But know this full well—in spite of all hell—
  Your *judgment* rests with yourself!

NECKED TRUTH

(For turk—human or animal)

Them that has—gets!
But gosh, by gee, by heck!—
He gets it, too, who hasn't a sou—
  He gets it—right in the neck!

ACCESSORIES BEFORE THE FACTS?

Are showy earrings
Just queer-rings
A woman wears
To distract the stares
From her nose, eyes and kissage
And the rest of her visage?

MISS UNDERSTANDING

"I want to scrutinize you, dear,"
He fondly to her said.
"How dare you, sir, you beastly cur!"
She cried and swiftly fled.

PAYS TO BE IGNORANT?

Yah, more an' more on less an' less
Of knowledge man's a glutton,
Until one day he may profess
To know ev'rything 'bout nuttin'!

TIMING RHYMING

"If Lincoln were alive today,
He'd likely be made president—
Of his Rail-Splitters' Union, say,"
Remarked a local resident.

SERENADE TO ARTIFICE

If her figure's bad, she's shrewdly garbed,
Her nose like a shad?—It's quickly barbed,
Where's the homely dear of yesteryear?

If she's too small, spikes never fail,
If she's too tall, flat heels prevail—
Where's the homely dear of yesteryear?

We spied a maid, looked like a vat—
Steam slimmed her down in nothing flat!
Another, who was mostly skin,
Is now shaped like a mandolin.

Like the dinosaur and mastodon
Have long since gone like Babylon,
The homely lass is now extinct,
(Or, p'raps we chaps, we saps, hoodwinked?)
But where's the homely dear of yesteryear?

CLUCK OF A PROUD LAMEDUCK

"I'm through with politics!" he said,
His manner it was grim.
He was not through with politics
For it was through with him!

ADD: AGENCY!

Advertising Agency,
You earn a hefty wage, and see
That we are briefed on each new gismo
From snoppygoops to clams from Pismo.

You sell smart slogans and fine phrases,
Your ingenuity amazes!
I've oft admired Mad'son Avenue,
Despite its hard cell, *have'n' you?*

MEDICALAGRAPH

Are medics sanguine (as they keep you waiting
As long as they jolly well please,)
That you'll catch from the other sick sister and brother
A much more costly disease?

PAGE HUMANITY

DOCTOR,
PROCTOR, lawyer
CROOK: Ev'ry man's a living
BOOK!

A ROSE IS—

"A primrose," says a wight who knows,
"Is but Miss Nomer for Miss Rose."

FOOD FOR THOUGHT

The Clarion Vegetarian:

". . . Have dominion over fish
. . . Over fowl of the air,
. . . Ev'ry [crawling] thing"
[We can shoot or snare!]

So says the Good Book,
But who wrote it, pray?
Egocentric man;
Then I, too, have my say:

Each living thing
Loves its life on this ball,
So, fie, fellow felons
And cannibals all!

The Non-Herbiverous Carniverous:

To which we "killers"
Make this reply:
"Don't slaughter a parsnip—
It, too, hates to die!"

CRACKED POTTAGE

(To P.M.)

"A psycho-ceramic", said a wit dynamic
Withal impish, blimpish, grim,
"Is surely, I wot, a mere crack-pot,
Or a kindly synonym."

4

Modern Mother Goose

Introduction

HISTORY OF THE MOTHER GOOSE FAMILY

. . . Many persons imagine that Mother Goose is a myth—that no such person ever existed. This is a mistake . . . Mother Goose was not only a veritable personage, but was born and resided many years in Boston, where many of her descendants may now be found.

. . . The family originated in England . . . came to this country . . . probably about the year 1656. . . . More than 200 years ago there was a small book in circulation in London bearing the name of "Rhymes for the Nursery" . . . which contained many of the identical pieces . . . in . . . the first book of its kind known to be printed in this country . . . by T. Fleet . . . Puddling Lane, 1719 Price, two coppers.

—Partial contents of a letter to the Boston Transcript circa 1830 signed "REQUIESCAT."

Hippie Mother Goose

BRED ON WELFARE BREAD

There was a young woman with her pad in a shoe,
Had so many children tho' she knew what to do,
Some called her a swinger, some called her a thief
Because the smart witch got rich on relief.

WHAT SEX, CURLY LOCKS?

"Curly Locks, Curly Locks,
Wilt thou be mine?
Thou shalt not wash dishes,
Thou shalt dine on wine."
But this scene today, I needs must deny,
For, curly locks could roof a chick or a guy.

ALL'S WELL THAT ENDS

Ding, dong, bell,
Percy's in the well.
What threw him in?
A pint of hippie gin.
What pulled him out?
A sniff of glue no doubt.

THE FLORAL UNMORAL

Are Flower Girls (unlaved, unshowered)
To vox a paradox—deflowered?

HIPPIEDROME

Hark! Hark! How their dogs do bark,
The hippies are barefooting to town,
Some in rags, some with jags,
Each bannering a four-letter noun!

BAN THE BANANA!

Tom-tom, the drummer's son
Stole a banana and away he run;
The fruit he smoked till he got coaked,
And this the son of a gun called fun!

DONNA BELLA SERENADE

Jacques and Zhill flew up the hill
To fetch more marijuana,
Fell off a bluff and lost the stuff,
So both sniffed belladonna.

RING-A-DING KING ON THE WING

Old King Cole was a merry old soul
And a merry, old soul was he:
And why was he so filled with glee?
He was also filled with L.S.D.!

DO AS ROMANS DO—AND DID!

"When in Rome," we hippies say,
"Have a Roman holiday!
"Fly off deep end, fly off handle!
"Be a roamin' Roman candle!"

HOW HUMPTY DUMPTY DUMPED

Humpty Dumpty sat on a wall,
Humpty Dumpty had a great Fall,
He had a great Winter, a Spring, Summer, too
Because he dug pot, what-not and glue.

CAVORT ANCIENT

She was a freak, he was a shriek:
Imagine! They danced *cheek to cheek!*

JACK WAS NO JUNKY DONKEY

"Jack be nimble,
Jack be quick,
Jack jump over
The candlestick!"
But Jack was no hippie
On a trip spree—
He lived in the days
Ere L.S.D.

MYTH IS GOOD AS A MILE

Youth more evil today is myth—
They've merely more tools to do it with.

HIPPIECULTURE VULTURE

"Mary, Mary, quite contrary,
How does your garden grow?"
"Poppy-seed and psychedelic weed,
And potted pot in a row."

MALODOROUS MELODY

Beautiful beads and blossoms, and bells,
Beautiful beads and blossoms, and bells,
Each bead count we like a rosaree,
While blossoms and bells drown out our smells.

NO SQUARE ROUND TRIPS

Jack Sprot would dig no pot,
His wife no seed or weed,
And so betwixt them both, I wot,
Sad squares they were indeed!

YIPPEE HIPPIE HIGH O

Joe, an unruly drop-out,
Flo, a truly knock out,
With greed would feed on weed and seed,
And make their friends' eyes pop out.

NOT GIRTH CONTROL

Jack and Jill
Once bought a pill;
Like 'twas no moral question,
For, (in big print:) 'twas SODA MINT,
'Cause Jill had indigestion.

KING HIPPIE THE 1ST

When hippies cool rule the world one day,
(The floral, amoral elves!)
They'll banish war forevermore,
For they'll never draft themselves!

PUMPKIN BUMPKIN

Peter, Peter, pumpkin eater,
Had a wife and always beat her.
"I like to smoke a gourd," she'd said.
Roared he: "(Biff!) Smoke a ham instead!"

HOT DOGGEREL

Bow, wow, wow,
Whose dog art thou?
Tommy Teener's own hot dog—
That's his fav'rite chow!

THE SCENE WAS JUMPING

Hey diddle, diddle,
The Cat and the Fiddle,
O'er the moon the cow jumped she,
The little dog did snort to spy such sport,
Like they all had L.S.D.

EVEN XANTIPPE WAS A HIPPIE

You may laugh at the Teeners,
Hip dances and wieners,
Their music, hamburgers and petting;
But try to be truthful,
You, too, were once youthful—
(Or does conscience make you forgetting?)

OF MICE & A MAN

Three Blind Mice,
See how they run!
But I learn they didn't
Run just for fun:
They were running away
From a square, I find,
Who talked them deaf
And dumb and *blind.*

MARI JUANA

Mary, Mary, you're quite contrary,
The way your garden breeds:
You once got your kick as a flower chick–
Now you cultivate the weeds!

WHAT RUB-A-DUB DUBS!

Rub-a-dub-dub, three men in a tub,
And if you dig that's bad,–
There were forty-five others, all good hippie brothers
Sharing their one-half room pad!

ALL COVERALLS AIN'T LEVIS

Homely she was and nearly neurotic
To the end of it's turning catastrophic,
But when she'd lay on the paint and crayon,
She soon was known as a hippie exotic.

THE GOOSE GOOSED

"Goosey, goosey gander, where shall I wander?
Upstairs and down stairs in my lady's chamber."

I knew a goose who tried it,
Has never denied it,
Now he's bruised and dotty,
'Cause the lady knew karati!

T.V. Radio Commercial Mother Goose

OLFACTORY VIRGIN

The maid was in the garden,
Hanging out the clothes;
Up came a little bird,
And snapt off her nose.

But the maid need not give it another thought. Dr. Rudolph Shnozzolnik, Plastic Surgeon, will snap it right back on the hapless virgin!

LITTLE BOY BLEW

Little Boy Blue, come blow your horn;
The sheep's in the meadow, the cow's in the corn.
Where's the little boy that looks after the sheep?
He's under the haycock, fast asleep.

Because the smart little master drinks Boval-tine—it travels the sleep faster!

LITTLE MISS MUFFED IT

Little Miss Muffet,
She sat on a tuffet,
Eating of curds and whey;
There came a great spider,
Who sat down beside her
And frightened Miss Muffet away,

—Quite an unnecessary flight, had she immediately phoned Ezmond's Exterminator Emporium. They let no spiders get tough with your tuffet, Miss Muffet!

JACK ASTERISK

Jack and Jill went up the hill
To fetch a pail of water;
Jack fell down and broke his crown,
And Jill came tumbling after

and needless to say both regretted to their dying day that they had not been insured by the Banana Royal Indemnity Company! Don't be a Jackass or a Jill! Insure against a spill!

WE SKIN YOU ALIVE, BABY BUNTING

Bye, Baby Bunting,
Father's gone a-hunting,
Mother's gone a-silking,
Brother's gone to buy a skin
To wrap the Baby Bunting in,

purchased from Beebelgeeber's Furre Shoppe, where we skin you from toe to toppe!

MOTHER HUBBARD'S DOG FOOD FOR THOT

Old Mother Hubbard
Went to the cupboard
To get her poor dog a bone;
But when she came there
The cupboard was bare,
And so the poor dog had none;

ah, but did the hapless woofer go nuts? Nay!—He'd laid by a big supply of Crunchley's Canine Doughnuts!

HUMPTY'S FRUIT

Humpty-dumpty sat on a wall,
Humpty-dumpty had a great fall

and are you aware that eggs are coming down, too, at the Super-Dooper Drive-in? Fresh crates are daily arrivin'!

JACK SPRATT PLATTERTUDE

Jack Spratt could eat no fat,
His wife could eat no lean;
And so betwixt them both, you see,
They licked the platter clean—

a most unnecessary maneuver: Deebo's Dandy Dishwasher will do it quick as a Hoover!

NIMBLE FOOTNOTE

Jack be nimble,
Jack be quick,
And Jack jump over the candlestick

by joining Geraldo's Giant Gymn to put you in trim!!!

WHO COCKED THE TRIGGER?

Who killed Cock Robin?
"I," said the Sparrow,
"With my bow and arrow,
I killed Cock Robin,

> but I must confess I attained my prowess at Mark Archery Park. Mark hits the mark!"

PUSSYFOOT WORK

Ding, dong bell,
Pussy's in the well,
Who put her een?
Little Tommy Green?
Who pulled her out?
Little Tommy Stout

> of the Tommy Stout Towing & Drayage Conveyage. We don't brag, but we sure got drag!

PIGGY R.F.D. P.D.Q.

To market, to market, to buy a fat pig,
Home again, home again, juggety jig.
To market, to market, to buy a fat hog.
Home again, home again, jiggety jog.

> Tsk! Tsk! Such excessive footwork! Dripper Dan, the Big Pork Man, *delivers* free with celeritee!

ST. IVES POPULATION BANG

As I was going to St. Ives,
I met a man with seven wives.
Every wife had seven sacks,

Every sack had seven cats,
Every cat had seven kits.
Kits, cats, sacks and wives,
How many were there going to St. Ives?

Cute! But difficult to compute? Then you've reckoned without Kounting's Klassy Kalculator. Moves swifter than the jaws of an alligator!

SUPPER SINGER'S SONG

Little Tommy Tucker
Sings for his supper;
What shall he eat?
White bread and butter.

How shall he cut it
Without e'er a knife?
How can he marry
Without e'er a wife?

Simply by applying at Hattie's Housewife Hacienda House. We supply the spouse. And we do cut the mustard; even the custard!

DILLEY OF A DOLLAR TIMEPIECE

A diller, a dollar, a ten o'clock scholar,
What makes you come so soon?
You used to come at ten o'clock,
But now you come at noon.

and if you're in this sad sack's plight, better buy a Halova Watch at Tick Tock Tommy's! Timepieces on tick. We have the pick!

TITTLEMOUSE'S FISH TALE

Little Tommy Tittlemouse
Lived in a little house,
He caught fishes
In other man's ditches,

but now he's as honest as any man—he buys sardines in the Bigge Yella Canne!

LULLABYEBYE

Come, let's to bed, says Sleepy-head;
Tarry a-while, says Slow;
Put on the pan, says Greedy Nan,
Let's sup before we go

on Shrentz's 97 Varieties—if only for the sake of variety. Endorsed by Society!

NEEDLE LESS PLIGHT

Needles and pins, needles and pins,
When a man marries, his trouble begins,

but no trouble whatsoever to buy his needles and pins by the book at Nyftie Netty's Notion Nook!

DIDDLE D.T.'S

Hey diddle, diddle, the cat and the fiddle,
The cow jumped over the moon;
The little dog laughed to see such sport,
And the dish ran away with the spoon—

if you, too, like the author of the foregoing, are in this wretched condition, or see pink polka-dotted mastadons, better buy a big bottle of Beppo's Bromo Burpo today! Chases those imps away!

MERRY MARY CONTRARY

Mary, Mary, quite contrary,
How does your garden grow?
Silver bells and cockle-shells,
And pretty maids all in a row,—

for, Mary's wide horticultural experience has made her wiser: she uses Foonigan's Fragrant Fertilizer. To be specific, it's terrific, prolific!

INSIDE STORY

I'll tell you a story
About Jack-a-Nory;
And now my story's begun.
I'll tell you another
About Jack and his brother;
And now my story's done;

but not quite. However, you can now read John-a-Nory's complete, unabridged, sensational deviate story in "Confidential Confessions." Rocking, socking, shocking!

PRESSING BUSINESS

Little Polly Flinders
Sat among the cinders,
Warming her pretty little toes.
Her mother came out and caught her
And whipped her little daughter
For spoiling her nice new clothes.

Fah! What a fatuous mater! She should have quickly dispatched Polly's habiliments to O'Googahan's Cleaning & Pressing Men! In business since Moses knows when!

HE SHOULD SHAVE A PIG!

Barber, barber shave a pig!
How many hairs will make a wig?
Four and twenty; that's enough,
Give the poor barber a pinch of snuff,

And remember—Dopenhagen's Snuff is the stuff!

CALLING MR. PORGIE

Georgie, Porgie, pudding and pie.
Kissed the girls and made them cry,
When the boys came out to play,
Georgie Porgie ran away,

But Mrs. Porgie: No need to get nervous; consult Googlepuffer's Skip Tracer's Service!

Red Mother Goose

LITTLE JEK HORNER

Little Jek Horner
Sat in the corner
Eating of caviar;
He poot in his thomb
And exploded a bomb—
He was framed 'cause he looked the tsar!

MY LITTLE RED HEN

Hickety, pickety, my red hen
She lays big eggs, now and then,
None for me and none for thee,
But ten for each of the commissar men.

TO MARKET, TO MARKET

To market, to market, to buy me some grog:
Some shots of good vodka, jiggedy-jog.
Home again, won't roam again—I'm full of lead
With no shots of vodka—they shot me instead!

THE CAPITALIST COW

The capitalist cow jumped over the moon,
De Milky Way to orbit;
I'll tell you why—she's a C.I.A. spy,
And de moon, you want to absorb it!

MADE IN U.S.S.R.

Hickery, dickery dock,
The mouse ran up the clock,
The clock struck once, it didn't strike twice—
Tsi! Tsi!—Imperial merchandise!

PIE-EYED PIPER

There was a piper had a cow,
On spoilt potatoes fed it,
But did it give a drop of milk?
Nyet and no—you sad it!

And so he pulled his bag pipes out
And sang to it a carol,
It still di'n't spill a gill of milk—
But vodka by the barrel!

SOVIET STYLE

Warsaw Margery Daw,
Sold her bed and lay on straw,
Was she poor and in despond?
Nyet! Matched her hair—*strawberry* blonde!

SIMPLE SIMON

Simple Simon met a spy man,
Who was on the peep;
Said Simple Simon to the spy man:
"I'll sell you secrets cheap."

Said the spy man to Simple Simon:
"Just what do you be knowing?"
Said Simple Simon to the spy man:
"Some roubles first be showing!"

Showed the spy man Simple Simon
Money by the carton,
Soon Simple Simon to the spy man
Secrets was impartin'.

Then clamped the spy man on Simple Simon
Bracelets made of iron,
Said Simple Simon to the spy man:
"Your joke I ain't admirin'!"

Said the spy man to Simple Simon:
"You're a cuckoo gremlin,
It's true that I, man, am a spy man—
A spy man for the Kremlin!"

But when the spy man nabbed poor Simon,
A laughing judge roared: *"Say, Gents,*
Tovariches the two are you—
You're *both* of you Red agents!"

VELL, I'LL TELL YOU—

I vood tell you a story
About Jack, the Knife gory,
  But sad vood be my fate:
First I'd be banished
And then vood have vanished,
  'Cause my story says, "Nots to the state!"

I could tell you another
About Jacknife's young brother,
  But vood not get very far
'Cause he lost his head
When they learned that he wed
  A ninety-foist coz' of the tsar!

RED VS. REDSKIN

Tom-Tom, the Sioux chief's son,
Stole a glance and away he run;
  Here we'd shoot the youth uncouth—
Russ Red justice can be fun!

WEE WILLIE WINKOFF

Wee Willie Winkoff
  Runs through the town
Upstairs and downstairs
  In his night-gown.
Wee Willie Winkoff
  Wasn't teched in hed—
The state repossessed
  His little rented bed.

RUSSIAN WOOF HOUNDS

Hark! Hark! De dogs do bark,
  De beggars are here in hysteria,
They're satellites, want equal rights,
  They'll get 'em—in Siberia!

JEK & JIL

Jek and Jil went up the hill
  Some vodka for to get,
The two young punks were delinquent drunks,
  So were shot in the Soviet.

MATA MARY, QUITE CONTRARY

Mata Mary quite contrary,
  Your garden's a flop, by Gemini!
Confess your guilt so you'll be kilt
  As a sabotaging enemy!

MY SON IVAN

Deedle, deedle dumpling, my son, Eevonne,
He vent to bed with both shoes on,
So you wonder why he didn't peel 'em—
He feared black marketeers would steal 'em!

OLD MUDDA HUBBARD

Old Mudda Hubbard
Vent to the cupboard
  To feed alien dog named Jones;
She was jailed in Pinsk by a cop named Minsk
  'Cause she ran a black market in bones.

THERE WAS A LITTLE GOIL

There was a little goil
And she wore a little coil
  Clear down to her natural stole-ah,
When she was good (or bad)
Her mama and her dad
  Bought her five dollar glass of Cola-Cola.

SHE LIVED IN A SHOE—NO HOUSING

There was an old woman
  Lived in a shoe,
With childrens, no housing—
  What else could she do?

She gave them some borsht
  And some heavy brown bread,
Stamped red stars on their heinies,
  Forty-five in a bed.

NO PARTY MEMBER

Heepetty hop to the barber shop
  To get a pot of *hot tea,*
But they said: "Nyet! No tea you get—
  You don't belong to The Potty."

COMMUNIST CALENDAR

Eighty days got September,
April, June and November—
  Maybe you think that I be wrong?

All the rest have sixty-two,
You say that ain't strictly true?
  (Life in Siberia seems that long!)

STAR SPY

Twinkle, twinkle, little star,
I don't vonder vot you are—
You're a Wall Street satellite,
Spying in our heavens bright.

You're a dastard, you're a knave
'Cause you seek but to enslave
In your armored chariot
Celestial proletariat!

GOOSEY GUSSIE GANDER

Agent Gussie Gander
Always loved to wander
  Up state and down state,
Full of propaganda.
Once she met an old man,
  A-sayin of his pray'rs,
So she threw him down the Russian Steppes
  (Their atheistic stairs).

PETER, BUMPKIN

Peter, Peter, a bumpkin eater,
Had a wife and couldn't keep her,
So, as an informer she got a job
And now *she* keeps the lazy old Slob.

PUSSYCAT PUSSYFOOT

Pasadena Pussyfoot
  Where have you been?
I've been to Moscow
  To see Lenin.

Pasadena Pussyfoot
What did you there?
I found a secret mike
'Neath my hotel room chair.

BEET BORSHT HOT

Beet borsht hot,
Beet borsht cold,
Beet borsht in the pot
Nine weeks old.
Invent some borsht
Without a beet
And we'll print your sit-meat
In Red Star concrete!

PETER PIPE-OFF

Peter Pipeoff peeked a peck of peekled pepper;
A peck of peekled pepper Peter Pipeoff picked,
If Peter Pipeoff peeked a peck of peekled pepper,
Where's the peck of peekled pepper Peter Pipeoff peeked?

By the state it was confiscated
And Peter was liquidated.
[*The saboteur should have peeked fo' pecks
And earned himself fo' kopeks!*]

JEK SPRATT

Jek Spratt could eat no fat,
His vife could eat no lean,
So they devoured "Das Kapital"
(There was no meat, I mean!)

LITTLE TOMSKI TUPPER

Little Tomski Tupper
Tried singing for his supper,
So what did he sing
For his black bread? (no butter):

Not a single note
Came from his throat;
He needed a plate,
(But couldn't afford an upper!)

HANDY SPANDY NOT SO DANDY

Handy-spandy, Jacky dandy
Loves plum-cake and sugar candy,
But in the shops they aren't so handy
So he had to settle for fish-cakes and brandy.

RED ST. IVES

As I was going to St. Ives,
I met seven wives,
Ev'ry wife had seven sacks,
Ev'ry sack had seven cats,
Ev'ry cat had seven kits,
So I have a notion
That an explosion
Of mom and pop-ulation
Likevise in Redland thrives.

The Bauhaus

Designed by Gillian Greenwood

Gillian Naylor

The Bauhaus

studio vista|dutton pictureback

General editor David Herbert

To Denny and Tom

Published in London by Studio Vista Limited
Blue Star House, Highgate Hill, N19
and in New York by E. P. Dutton and Co. Inc.
201 Park Avenue South, New York, NY 10003
Distributed in Canada by General Publishing Co Limited
30 Lesmill Road, Don Mills, Toronto, Ontario
Set in 8D on 9 pt Univers, 2 pts leaded
Made and printed in Great Britain by
Richard Clay (The Chaucer Press), Ltd, Bungay, Suffolk

SBN 289 37047 7 (cased)
289 37048 5 (paperback)

Contents

Sources

The Bauhaus was founded in April 1919; for the next fourteen years its existence was threatened by shortage of funds, hostile officials and internal feuds. When it was finally closed down by the Nazis in 1933 it had moved three times, and had produced less than 500 graduates. Yet even in its brief lifetime the Bauhaus had become a legend, and now, some fifty years after its foundation it still remains a symbol of a progressive attitude to architecture and design. For the school set out, in a resurgence of optimism and idealism after the First World War, to train a generation of architects and designers to accept and anticipate the demands of the twentieth century; and to use all its resources, technical, scientific, intellectual and aesthetic, to create an environment that would satisfy man's spiritual as well as his material needs. How far it achieved these aims is a matter of conjecture, for the Bauhaus was cut off before it had time either to consolidate or betray its early ideals. Its foundation, however, is a milestone in the history of man's efforts to come to terms with technology; for in spite of its inconsistencies, both ideological and practical, the Bauhaus did more than any other organization, either in the nineteenth or twentieth centuries, to reconcile man and his man-made environment.

During the fourteen years of its existence the Bauhaus was to change its character many times; as Gropius pointed out: 'Ideas of cultural import cannot spread and develop any faster than the society which they seek to serve.' [1] The establishment of a valid curriculum for a school that was to 'restore the idea of the fundamental unity underlying all branches of design',[2] and 'create type-forms that would meet all technical, aesthetic and commercial demands' [3] was a long and sometimes painful process. In order to effect the transition from nineteenth-century to twentieth-century attitudes, Gropius enlisted the help of *avant garde* artists such as Feininger, Klee, Kandinsky and Moholy-Nagy; it was their function to create and stimulate the creative process; and their attitudes to shape, colour, space and form had a profound influence on the work of the Bauhaus. The school was to a certain extent, however, founded in a spirit of nineteenth-

Cherwell Cotton velvet printed from Morris's design *c.* 1885

century nostalgia, a nostalgia that is reflected in the tone of Gropius's proclamation to announce its opening: 'Let us create a new *guild of craftsmen*, without the class distinctions which raise an arrogant barrier between craftsman and artist. Together, let us conceive and create the new building of the future, which will embrace architecture *and* sculpture *and* painting in one unity and which will one day rise toward heaven from the hands of a million workers, like the crystal symbol of a new faith.' [4]

Taken at their face value, these words could well have been written fifty years earlier by William Morris, and the conflicting ideologies that threatened the Bauhaus in its early years were in part a hangover from nineteenth-century controversies on the nature of art, education and industry, and in part the result of a certain ambiguity in Gropius's attitude. For, although with his Fagus and Werkbund exhibition factories he had established a new standard in industrial architecture, his attitude to industrial design, in the early 'twenties at least, was conditioned by the ideals of a long line of reformers who 'strove to find a means of reuniting the world of art with the world of work'.[5] In order, therefore, to understand the aims of the school in Weimar, and to appreciate its subsequent achievements in Dessau, it is necessary to trace briefly the development of these nineteenth-century attitudes.

The implications of mechanization had preoccupied architects and social commentators throughout the century. In England, the first country to feel the effects of the Industrial Revolution, an artistic élite thundered against the invasion of industry; and while Telford, Brunel and Paxton were creating a new aesthetic vocabulary in iron and glass, the 'official' architects preferred to follow Ruskin in his belief that greatness lay in the reconstruction of past forms: 'We want no new style of architecture . . . The forms of architecture already known to us are good enough for us, and far better than any of us.' [6] This flight from reality was reinforced by the traditional methods of instruction in art academies throughout Europe, where the slavish imitation of past styles was never questioned.

Even before 1850, however, there were a few realists in artistic circles. In 1847 Henry Cole had founded a firm called Summerly's Art Manufactures in an attempt to persuade painters and sculptors

Pewter clock with copper face, numbers and hands, Charles Annesley Voysey, 1903

Silver porringer, set with semi-precious stones, C. R. Ashbee, *c.* 1900 *Victoria and Albert Museum, Crown copyright reserved*

Sussex chair Morris & Co, 1865. *Victoria and Albert Museum, Crown copyright reserved*

to produce designs for manufactured goods; in 1849 he began with his colleagues, Richard Redgrave, Matthew Digby Wyatt and Owen Jones, to publish a *Journal of Design and Manufactures* with the same aim of setting out standards for industry to follow. He was a member of the executive committee that organized the Great Exhibition of 1851, and he was ruthless in his condemnation of the goods that were displayed there. Later, as secretary of the Department of Science and Art, he was in charge of the Schools of Design in South Kensington, where he attempted to introduce practical methods of instruction.

Throughout the rest of the century in England there were other men who, like Cole, attempted to inject 'art' into industry, but they were overshadowed by the larger-than-life figure of William Morris, who towers like a colossus, dominating the nineteenth-century scene. Morris loathed the values of the steam age as much as Ruskin and his followers, but his condemnation was backed by a highly developed social conscience. He believed in the artist's responsibility to society, and in the possibility of improving man by improving his environment. Art and beauty, according to Morris, need not be confined to painting and sculpture; all men, he maintained, should be able to furnish their homes with products created by a 'decorative, noble, *popular* art', and he envisaged a time when 'in no private dwelling will there be any signs of waste, pomp or insolence, and every man will have his share of the *best*'.[7]

Interior by Charles Annesley Voysey, *c.* 1900

The best, however, could only be created by a dedicated craftsman, working directly with his materials. Nothing of value could be produced by machinery, since mass production brought with it mass degradation: 'Men living among such ugliness cannot conceive of beauty, and therefore cannot express it.' [8]

Morris, therefore, rejected the machine on social as well as aesthetic grounds, and spent his life trying to re-establish the values of the medieval world, as he saw them, in nineteenth-century England. In his wake came a whole generation of designer/craftsmen who revived the decorative arts to such an extent that in Germany in the eighteen-seventies 'national lamentations were to be heard concerning the importation of English material for decoration', and *le style anglais* became all the rage in Paris. 'When English creations began to appear,' wrote Samuel Bing, an art dealer and entrepreneur who was one of the first to promote *L'Art Nouveau* in his shop in Paris, 'a cry of delight sounded throughout Europe. Its echo can still be heard in every country.' [9]

These English 'creations'—wallpapers and textiles, silverware, jewelry and some furniture, were the work of highly sophisticated craftsmen (many of them were architects)—men like Arthur Heygate Mackmurdo, Heywood Sumner, Charles Annesley Voysey and Charles Robert Ashbee, who throughout the latter part of the nineteenth century formed guilds, societies and artistic communities in order to produce their designs and promote their ideas.

They were soon well known on the Continent, for their work was illustrated in the various art magazines that were established in the eighteen-nineties, and they were invited to contribute to exhibitions held in Belgium, France, Germany and Austria, which in themselves were a manifestation of the revived interest in the 'applied arts'. Their design philosophy, however, made as great an impact as their work, for these British designers had inherited Morris's social conscience as well as his preoccupation with beauty, nature and fitness for purpose. Although their designs (especially the wallpapers, textiles, silverware and book illustrations) were an inspiration to many of the Continental designers associated with Art Nouveau, the British craftsmen tended to hold themselves aloof from what Walter Crane called 'that strange decorative disease', with the result that Continental designers and their patrons looked again at what Britain had to offer when they began to react against a style that had become purely decorative.

Germany, for example, had many links with England throughout the nineteenth century. Gottfried Semper, a German architect and theorist, had lived in London from 1850–5; he became associated with Henry Cole and his circle and joined them in condemning the standard of the exhibits in the Great Exhibition of 1851. His thoughts on this exhibition prompted him to write *Wissenschaft, Industrie und Kunst,* which was published in 1852. In this prophetic book Semper describes and condemns the divorce between industry and craftsmanship which had been accompanied by a general lowering of aesthetic standards. Nothing of value, he maintained, would be achieved in either sphere, until this gulf was bridged. During his stay in London, Semper was a political exile and his theories found few sympathizers in either country at that time. Forty years later, however, German politicians and industrialists as well as architects were extremely interested in British achievements, and in 1896 the Prussian Board of Trade decided to send an official representative to London in order to report on the success of British architecture and design. Hermann Muthesius spent several years in London and he returned to Germany with new ideals for domestic architecture and a belief in the potentials of machine production.

He was excited and impressed by what he saw in England. On the one hand, architects like Philip Webb, Norman Shaw and C. F. A. Voysey, inspired by Morris, had brushed aside the dead hand of historicism and had created a new style of domestic architecture, and on the other the nineteenth-century engineers had demonstrated what could be achieved with iron and steel, concrete and glass, the raw materials of the industrial age. Out of these elements, simplicity in domestic architecture and a sympathetic use of the machine, a new style, according to Muthesius, could be created.

On his return to Germany in 1903 he began to publicize his ideas in a series of lectures, books and pamphlets. These reveal him as a far greater realist than any of the English designers he so admired. For as a civil servant with a special brief to improve his country's trading position, he could never take up ivory tower

Chair for a music room, Richard Riemerschmid, *c.* 1899

attitudes to machine production; Muthesius was convinced that the disciplines of industry and craftsmanship could be combined, and he set about forging the links.

He was outspoken in his condemnation of current complacency, both on the part of industry and the German craft organizations, and he made enemies in both camps. However, his position carried a great deal of weight. As head of the Prussian Board of Trade for Schools of Art and Crafts he controlled the appointments to art schools, and he made sure that men who were sympathetic to his ideas got the most important posts. In 1903, the architect Hans Poelzig was made principal of the art academy in Breslau; at the same time Bruno Paul became director of the art school in Berlin, and Peter Behrens was appointed head of the Düsseldorf school of art. All three were architects of some standing, experimenting in their buildings with the engineering aesthetic of steel, concrete and glass that Muthesius so admired. In addition Bruno Paul and Peter Behrens were both to be associated with German industry's earliest attempts to work with designers.

The first moves in this direction came in 1905 when Karl Schmidt, a Dresden cabinet maker, had asked his brother-in-law, a young architect named Richard Riemerschmid, to design him a chair that could be produced in his workshop 'developing the style from the spirit of the machine'. In 1907 Schmidt commissioned

Glasses and carafe by Richard Riemerschmid, *c.* 1905

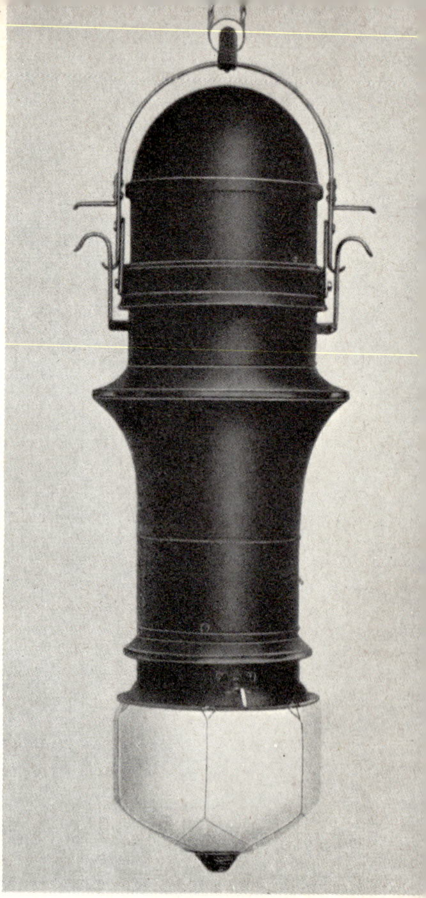

Lamps by Peter Behrens for AEG, *c*. 1910

Bruno Paul to design him a range of low cost furniture for mass production, and in that same year AEG, the electrical combine, had appointed Peter Behrens as their design consultant. In this capacity Behrens acted as architect to the group, designing the famous Turbine Factory of 1908, as well as street lamps, light fittings and publicity material.

Place setting by Richard Riemerschmid; made by P. Bruckmann & Sohne, *c.* 1912

The year 1907 is one of the most significant in the history of industrial design, for with Behrens' appointment to AEG the design profession was established, and in the same year Muthesius announced the formation of the Deutscher Werkbund, the first of many societies which subsequently sprang up throughout Europe to improve standards in design and industry. Unlike the British guilds and craft societies of the nineteenth century the Werkbund was, from the outset, an association of *manufacturers*, architects and craftsmen. Its aims, laid down in its statutes, were to unite 'artists, craftsmen, experts and patrons, intent on an improvement of production through the collaboration of art, industry and the crafts'.

For the next seven years, therefore, German architects were consolidating these first tentative links with industry, and the yearbooks of the Deutscher Werkbund, published between 1912 and 1915, give a good picture of developments, both theoretical and practical, in German architecture and industrial design. The illustrations of consumer goods, for example, reflect the conflicting attitudes of designers at that time, for a coherent style was slow to emerge. Some designers found that the links with the past were hard to break, and there are reminiscences of Jugendstil, the German equivalent of Art Nouveau, as well as ample evidence of the florid, highly decorative style that Muthesius was trying to banish. This conflict of ideologies was also extended to design and architectural theory; the individualists, championed by Henry van de Velde, the Belgian architect, at that time head of the Weimar School of Arts and Crafts, believed that design was a personal process, and that the artist should never be forced to submit to rules. Muthesius, however, maintained that machine production demanded standardization (*Typisierung*), which involved working to precise formulae, as in Classical architecture. This clash of opinion came to a head in 1914 when Werkbund members were preparing for an important exhibition in Cologne. In a series of speeches they defined their attitudes. Muthesius declared: 'Architecture and with it the Werkbund moves towards standardization . . . Only standardization . . . can once again introduce a universally valid, self confident taste.' Van de Velde, counter-attacking, replied: 'As long as there are artists in the Werkbund . . . they are going to protest against any

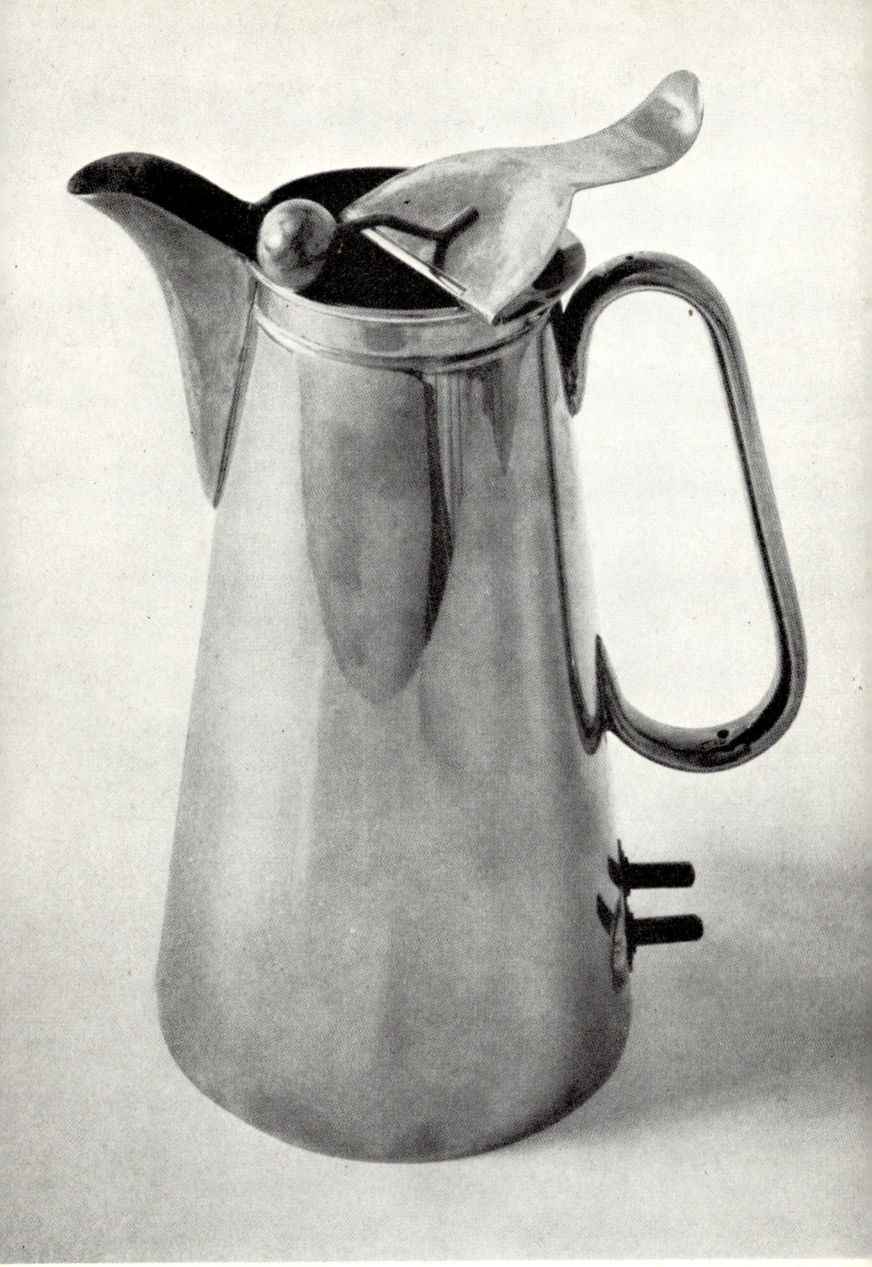

Jug by Peter Behrens for AEG, *c.* 1910

suggestion of a canon of standardization, the artist is essentially a free, spontaneous creator. He will never voluntarily submit to a discipline forcing on him a type or canon.'

The exhibition itself, however, was a triumph for the Werkbund, and several of the buildings there demonstrated that at last a style appropriate to contemporary technology had been achieved. One was a pavilion for the glass industry designed by Bruno Taut, and the others were a model factory, Halle des Machines, and administrative block designed by Walter Gropius and his partner, Adolf Meyer. Three years earlier Gropius and Meyer had built the Fagus factory at Alfeld-an-der-Leine, and with these two buildings Gropius emerged as one of the leading architects of the twentieth century.

Dining room chair in mahogany, Walter Gropius, 1913 *Photograph courtesy Walter Gropius*

Mahogany cabinet, Walter Gropius, 1913 *Photograph courtesy Walter Gropius*

But although by 1911 Gropius had established a new language of industrial architecture, it was many years before he was able to achieve a similar breakthrough in product design. Prior to 1914 Germany had done more than any other country to achieve some form of collaboration between the crafts and industry, but in the Bauhaus Gropius was attempting to create a new profession to serve a new kind of society. In order to do this he had to transcend nineteenth-century romanticism, resolve the conflict between 'spontaneity' and 'standardization', and redefine his attitudes to the role of art and technology in society. He was faced with the reality of the twentieth century, and in the Bauhaus he attempted to establish disciplines to meet these realities. These were gradually determined as the Bauhaus faced crisis after crisis, and the battles that were fought there have not yet been won.

Administration building for the Werkbund Exhibition, Cologne; Walter Gropius with Adolf Meyer, 1914. *Photograph courtesy Walter Gropius*

Detail of staircase, administrative building, Werkbund Exhibition, Cologne 1914.
Photograph courtesy Walter Gropius

Walter Gropius

The Ideals . . . 1907–1918

In 1914 when it was first suggested that he might take over the arts and crafts school in Weimar, Gropius was thirty-one; he was the son of an architect, and great nephew of Martin Gropius, who had been an architect of some standing in the nineteenth century (he designed the Museum of Arts and Crafts in Berlin, and in 1867 was appointed principal of the Arts and Crafts School in that city, as well as director of art education for Prussia).

Walter Gropius studied architecture in Berlin and Munich, but his practical training began in 1907 when he joined the office of Peter Behrens. He could not have found a more stimulating environment at that time, for Behrens had just begun to work for AEG, and was involved in product and graphic design as well as architecture. His office was a training ground for some of the most influential architects of the next generation; soon after Gropius's appointment the young Mies van der Rohe joined the

Damask wall fabric, Walter Gropius, 1913 *Photograph courtesy Walter Gropius*

Opposite:
Wardrobe in white enamelled poplar, Walter Gropius, 1913 *Photograph courtesy Walter Gropius*

staff, and Le Corbusier also spent some months there. In his book *The New Architecture and the Bauhaus*, first published in 1935, Gropius acknowledges his debt to Behrens: 'In 1908, when I finished my preliminary training and embarked on my career as an architect with Peter Behrens, the prevalent conception of architecture and architectural education were still entirely dominated by the academic stylization of the classical "Orders". It was Behrens who first introduced me to logical and systematical co-ordination in the handling of architectural problems. In the course of my active association with the important schemes on which he was then engaged, and frequent discussions with him and other prominent members of the Deutscher Werkbund, my own ideas began to crystallize as to what the essential nature of building ought to be. I became obsessed by the conviction that modern constructional technique could not be denied expression in architecture, and that that expression demanded the use of unprecendented forms.'

In translating these theories on architecture into practice, even in these early years, Gropius went further than Behrens, for in spite of his pioneering role, Behrens himself never entirely succeeded, prior to the First World War, in breaking away from the classical tradition in architecture. His Turbine Factory of 1908–9, for example, was the first German building to make extensive use of glass and steel, but in basic form it remains pseudo-classic. Gropius on the other hand began even at the outset of his career, to demonstrate his ability to grasp the potentials of the new materials and techniques that were becoming available to architects, and to suggest completely new ways of using them. He was also, from the outset of his career, preoccupied with the architect's social responsibilities. As early as 1909, for example, he had sent a memorandum to Emil Rathenau, President of AEG, outlining the advantages of using prefabricated units in housing construction: 'The idea of industrializing house construction can be realized by the repetition in each building of the same standard component parts. This would mean that mass production methods could be employed which would be cheaper for the producer and could result in lower rents for the occupiers . . . It is possible to have an infinite number of variations of every plan type by differing combinations of the standard elements.'[10]

Gropius was anticipating the preoccupations of twentieth-century planners when he wrote this. He was also ahead of his time, when, on leaving Behrens to set up his own practice, he designed the Fagus factory of 1911, and the factory for the 1914 Werkbund exhibition, for in both these buildings he uses glass and steel as no architect had used it before. The façade of the main block of the Fagus factory was faced with a 'curtain' of glass, supported by narrow steel mullions. In order to emphasize the transparency of the structure there were no supports at the corners—a complete innovation at that time. Similarly in the Werkbund factory, the staircases at each end of the main administration block are enclosed in circular glass towers so that the internal structure is exposed. In both these buildings Gropius was anticipating design and construction methods that were not fully developed until the 'thirties; in his product design at that time, however, and in his theoretical writings, he does not venture beyond the standards set by the Werkbund. Two articles he wrote for its yearbooks in

Fagus shoe-last factory, Alfeld-an-der-Leine, Walter Gropius with Adolf Meyer, 1911 *Photograph courtesy Walter Gropius*

Opposite:
Corner detail, Fagus factory

Entrance to Fagus factory

Machine workshop, Fagus factory

1913 and 1914 show him firmly committed to the development of a modern industrial architecture, but at the same time his ideas on how to improve standards in industrial production are closely identified with those of contemporary reformers. Like Muthesius he believed that the *artist* possessed the power to 'breathe life into the dead product of the machine', and that 'the sensibility of the artist must be combined with the knowledge of the technician to create new forms in architecture and design'.

Diesel locomotive for the railway factory, Königsberg, 1913. *Photograph courtesy Walter Gropius*

Another view of diesel locomotive shown on preceding page

Opposite:

Sleeping car for the railway factory, Königsberg, 1913 *Photograph courtesy Walter Gropius*

Ideas such as these were generally accepted in the Germany of 1914, and they made him a natural successor to Henry van de Velde when the latter resigned as principal of the Weimar School of Art and Crafts.

Van de Velde, a Belgian architect, had been working in Germany since the turn of the century, and in 1902 he had been appointed artistic adviser to the Grand Duke of Saxe-Weimar, one of several German princes, who by their patronage of the arts and local industries, contributed to the revival that was to lead to the formation of the Werkbund.

Van de Velde was born in 1863, and had begun his career as a painter. He was, however, 'converted' to design and architecture in his early twenties when he discovered the work of Morris and his circle. By the eighteen-nineties he was well known throughout Europe as an architect and designer in the Art Nouveau tradition, but even while he was still associated with Art Nouveau, his imagination was fired by the power and potential of the machine. In a series of lectures published in 1902 and 1903 he defined his position. Machinery inspired him with a kind of aesthetic awe, but at the same time he recognized its social value. By rejecting machine techniques the English arts and crafts designers had produced work that only a rich and cultured élite could afford, but according to van de Velde, the machine, properly used, could bring about a revolution in architecture and design. Anticipating the ideals of the Werkbund he demanded 'a logical structure of products, uncompromising logic in the use of materials, proud and frank exhibition of working processes'.[11]

His opinions and his work were highly thought of in Germany, and the post he was offered in Weimar gave him the opportunity to put his ideals into practice. Soon after his arrival there he established workshops in the existing School of Fine Art, and in 1902 he decided to open a private craft school where students were encouraged to develop an intuitive approach in order to create new forms, rather than relying on traditional solutions. Several small scale industries flourished in Weimar at that time and the school was able to establish links with local manufacturers. Their work, however, was firmly based on craft techniques, and in promoting this approach, van de Velde was being realistic rather than reactionary. For the jewelers, metalworkers,

Folkwang Museum, Hagen, Henry van de Velde, 1901–2

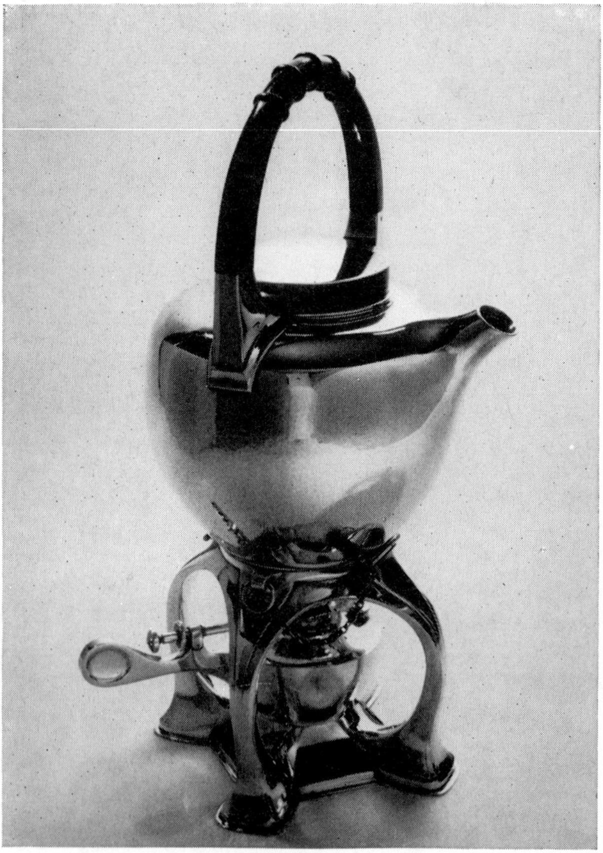

Silver samovar, Henry van de Velde, 1902–3 *Kunstgewerbemuseum, Zurich*

Chair by Henry van de Velde, 1900

Candlesticks and dish, Henry van de Velde, 1914 *Folkwang Museum, Essen*

cabinet makers and wood workers of Weimar had never become highly mechanized, and the Industrial Revolution, which had so debased British output, had hardly touched them. Under this régime the school flourished and eventually van de Velde persuaded the Grand Duke to take it over, so that in 1908 it became the state-owned *Grossherzogliche Kunstgewerbeschule* (School of Arts and Crafts).

In the years leading up to 1914, however, van de Velde's influence in Weimar began to wane. The Grand Duke, who had a somewhat volatile nature, was losing interest in the school, and, in an excess of nationalism, 'foreign' designers and artists became suspect. Van de Velde handed in his resignation in 1914, and at the same time recommended three possible successors—August Endell, Hermann Obrist and Walter Gropius.

Gropius was the youngest of the contenders (Obrist was 51 in 1914 and Endell was 43), and he was asked to work in Weimar; it was never quite clear, however, throughout the war, what position he would hold there. Soon after van de Velde had hinted to Gropius that he was in the running for the post, the Grand Duke, with characteristic abruptness, had closed down the school completely, and had dismissed the staff. Fortunately, however, various officials within the Weimar government were opposed to this move, and with the support of Fritz Mackensen, director of the Weimar Academy of Fine Art, they began negotiations to continue the craft school as a department within the academy, and at the same time to open a school of architecture there. Details of the vague, but complex negotiations that followed are revealed in the correspondence and documents in Hans Wingler's *Das Bauhaus*.[12]

These demonstrate Gropius's ability as a negotiator, and his determination to run things his own way. Mackensen had suggested that the combined school of architecture and craft should be under the direction of Gropius, while he (Mackensen) remained principal of the whole organization. Gropius, however, attempted to obtain a clear-cut ruling about his own position. In a letter dated 19 October 1915 he writes: 'I still feel the need for more positive proposals on the nature of these links with the academy, and on the *independence* of the school of architecture. You spoke in your letter of a small independent school . . . I am unable to grasp, however, what my position as head of the school of architecture would entail; furthermore I cannot envisage teaching architecture as a separate entity, since architecture is all embracing. What I have in mind is an independent teaching organization, which must necessarily develop from small beginnings, and which could be co-ordinated with the existing academy for administrative and technical purposes, but which, from the artistic point of view, must remain *independent*. If I am to work profitably I must be allowed to develop my own ideas on fundamental issues—*freedom of action* must be an essential condition . . .' A few months later, after further negotiations with the Grand Duke, Gropius redefined his aims for the school in a long and detailed memorandum. Extracts from this important document were published for the first time in Wingler's book, and it is interesting to compare Gropius's proposals at that time with his far more ambitious and idealistic programme once the Bauhaus was established.

In the memorandum of 1914 Gropius repeats, sometimes word for word, the ideas he set out in his two Werkbund articles. He describes the schism that had arisen between the artist, the craftsman and industry, and the attempts at reform that had already taken place. It was no longer sufficient, he maintained, to be concerned with handwork, and with the output of small firms, since these had never completely lost touch with 'art'. The artist must learn to become directly involved in mass production, and the industrialist must be taught to accept the artist and his values. Gropius then goes on to suggest a programme of education that would 'create a situation in which the artist would come to terms with the most powerful means of modern production, the machine, from the simplest tool to the most specialised machinery'. To achieve this end he visualized a school that would be closely linked with local industries and workshops. These would send their most promising apprentices, selected in consultation with instructors at the school. The courses would consist of practical work, studies in form and composition, as well as art history and theory; for those who were technically rather than artistically gifted there would be lessons in technical and free drawing. Students who had attended the courses would form the nucleus of a 'happy working community, such as had existed in an ideal way in the masons' lodges of the Middle Ages'; by adapting the working methods of the Middle Ages to present-day requirements they would help to create the right conditions for the emergence of a new style.

It is, of course, difficult to reconcile the fact of the Fagus factory, which made so uncompromising a break with past styles, techniques and materials, with this talk of guilds, happy bands of craftsmen and medieval cathedrals. Gropius was, however, throughout his career, to draw parallels between the medieval ideal and his own conception of the architect's role in society. 'The new building of the future, which will embrace architecture *and* sculpture *and* painting' (1919) becomes in 1923 'the composite but inseparable work of art, the great building in which the old dividing line between monumental and decorative elements would have disappeared altogether'. He returns to the theme thirty years later. In an article reprinted in *The Scope of Total Architecture* Gropius describes teaching his Harvard students how to 'collaborate without losing their identity' and continues: 'In our particular field there is no book of rules for such a collaboration, unless we go back as far as the Middle Ages to study the working teams of the great cathedral builders. Most striking within the organization of these building guilds was the fact that until the late eighteenth century every craftsman in the job was not an executing hand only, but was permitted to put his own design into his part of the work as long as he abided by the master's guiding key of design, which was the secret geometrical auxiliary of the building guilds, similar to the keys in musical composition. Preconceived paper design hardly existed at all; the group lived together, discussed the task and built their ideas.'

It is the corporate approach to design and architecture which implies teamwork, standardization and modular co-ordination (the twentieth-century equivalent of the 'master's guiding key'), that Gropius was trying to convey at the Bauhaus and later at Harvard. For him the medieval cathedral epitomized such an approach with architect, wood carvers, stone carvers and masons all working together to achieve a corporate vision.

Gropius himself had no difficulty in relating this vision to the demands of the twentieth-century, but his theories were open to misinterpretation, especially in those first years at Weimar when Bauhaus students were bitterly debating their role in society. Gradually, however, these essentially nineteenth-century ideals took on a new dimension, and the Bauhaus was finally able to relate them to the new vision which Gropius was convinced could and must be taught in an age of technology.

Between 1914 and 1919, however, his ideas on how it should

be taught changed completely. His suggestions in the memorandum are down to earth and practical, but Gropius was, in effect, proposing an intensification of the methods already practised in Germany's schools of art and crafts. The 1914 memorandum was the logical culmination of all the efforts, throughout the past seventy years, to improve the standard and status of mass produced goods, and to train 'artists' to work with industry.

The next four years, however, were to change the face of Europe. Germany had lost a generation, and in the revolutions that followed the war, those who survived attempted to establish a new social and political order. In spite of the country's humiliation and defeat, its intellectuals were seized with the fervour of reform and, for a brief period the most radical of the reformers were a group of artists, architects and poets, who, inspired by the new ideas that had swept in from Russia, Paris, Italy and Holland, decided to take advantage of the temporary rout of bourgeois values in order to build a new world.

Gropius spent the months following the armistice in Berlin, which rapidly became a centre of this artistic/socialist activity. He was caught up in the turmoil of art movements, and he joined the Novembergruppe, a society named after the month of the Weimar Revolution. Its members included the painters Lyonel Feininger and Karl Schmidt-Rottluff, the sculptor Gerhard Marcks and the architects Mies van der Rohe, Erich Mendelsohn, Hans Poelzig and Bruno Taut. They all became identified with Expressionism, a romantic movement of protest—protest against accepted values in art, architecture and society, which had led to the degradation of man's essential humanity; and by means of exhibitions, pamphlets and manifestoes, the group tried to demonstrate how it would build a new world out of the shattered remnants of the old.

The war and the attitudes of his contemporaries obviously had a profound effect on Gropius; his idealism was intensified ('There are no architects today', he wrote in a prospectus for an exhibition of the Novembergruppe, 'we are all preparing the way for the one who some day will merit this name again. That name implies "Master of the Art", one who will make gardens out of deserts, and let miracles rise to the sky'), but it also strengthened his sense of responsibility to his own and future generations.

In *The New Architecture and the Bauhaus* he describes his state of mind at this time, 'The full consciousness of my responsibility in advancing ideas based on my own reflections only came home to me as a result of the war . . . After that violent interruption, which kept me, like most of my fellow architects, from work for four years, every thinking man felt the necessity for an intellectual change of heart. Each in his own particular sphere of activity aspired to help in bridging the disastrous gulf between reality and idealism. It was then that the immensity of the mission of the architects of my own generation first dawned on me. I saw that an architect cannot hope to realize his ideas unless he can influence the industry of his country sufficiently for a new school of design to arise as a result; and unless that school succeeds in acquiring authoritative significance. I saw, too, that to make this possible would require a whole staff of collaborators and assistants: men who would work, not automatically as an orchestra obeys its conductor's baton, but independently, although in close co-operation, to further a common cause.'

Weimar

To put his ideas into practice, therefore, Gropius needed to establish an entirely new kind of school of architecture and design. The ideal raw material was there, in Weimar, but the situation after the war was so confused that he did not know whether or not there would be a post for him. Ducal rule had ended with the revolution of 1918, the school of arts and crafts was closed, Mackensen had resigned as principal of the Academy of Fine Arts, and it was not clear who had the authority to make new appointments.

It is important to outline briefly the complex negotiations that took place at this time, for they contributed to the controversies that were eventually to close the school in Weimar. The documents published, many of them for the first time, in Wingler's *Das Bauhaus*, relate the course of events, and reveal Gropius's capacity to cut through confusion and compromise to achieve his own ends.

As soon as the war was over Gropius began to seek confirmation of his appointment, and in January 1919 he wrote to Freiherr von Fritsch, then Lord Chamberlain in Weimar, reminding him of his pre-war correspondence and meetings with the Grand Duke and his ministers. Von Fritsch then made enquiries about Gropius and received favourable answers; the staff at the academy declared themselves in his favour, and the trade and industry association in Weimar recalled Mackensen's earlier suggestion that a school of arts and crafts should be established within the academy, under the direction of Gropius. Encouraged by all these expressions of faith in Gropius, the Lord Chamberlain exercised his by then somewhat nebulous powers and confirmed the appointment. This was on 16 March 1919; on 20 March Gropius applied for and received permission to rename the combined schools *das Staatliches Bauhaus*; his appointment was signed in April and later in the same month the famous manifesto appeared in the German newspapers and was circularized to the art schools: 'The complete building is the final aim of the visual arts. Their noblest function was once the decoration of buildings. Today they exist in isolation, from which they can be rescued only through the

Bathers oil, Lyonel Feininger, 1912 *Photograph courtesy Busch-Reisinger Museum*

conscious co-operative effort of all craftsmen. Architects, painters and sculptors must recognize anew the composite character of a building as an entity. Only then will their work be imbued with the architectonic spirit which it has lost as "salon art".

'Architects, sculptors, painters, we must all turn to the crafts.

'Art is not a "profession". There is no essential difference between the artist and the craftsman. The artist is an exalted craftsman. In rare moments of inspiration, moments beyond the control of his will, the grace of heaven may cause his work to blossom into art. *But proficiency in his craft is essential to every artist.* Therein lies a source of creative imagination.

'Let us create a new guild of craftsmen, without the class distinctions which raise an arrogant barrier between craftsman and artist. Together let us conceive and create the new building of the future, which will embrace architecture *and* sculpture *and* painting in one unity and which will rise one day toward heaven from the hands of a million workers like the crystal symbol of a new faith.' [13]

While Lyonel Feininger's cathedral woodcut which accompanied this declaration symbolized the Expressionist aspirations of the new school, its programme described a course that was down to earth and practical. This was aimed at destroying the traditional apartheid between artist, architect, craftsman and industry, but by this time Gropius had abandoned the idea of gradually achieving such a fusion by taking in apprentices from local factories. Students of all ages and nationalities were invited to apply for the course, which was to be completely unacademic. 'The school is the servant of the workshop; and the day will come when the school will be absorbed into the workshop.' [14] In order to stress the differences between this and all former art schools, the professorial titles were dropped and the terminology of the medieval guilds revived. There were to be no 'students' and

Cover for Bauhaus proclamation, woodcut on coloured paper, Lyonel Feininger, 1919 *Photograph courtesy Busch-Reisinger Museum*

'teachers' at the school, but 'masters', 'journeymen' and 'apprentices'. These would work together on joint projects, and at the same time every student would be encouraged to discover and develop his individual potential.

This programme attracted students from all over Germany; their ages ranged from seventeen to forty years and at least half of the men had been at the front. The majority were penniless (Gropius was later able to persuade the Ministry of Education in Weimar to cancel tuition fees), but they were all in those grim post-war years seeking a Cause and a Community, and this was what the Bauhaus gave them. A former student writes: 'My economic future was far from secure, but I decided to join the Bauhaus. It was during the post-war years, and to this day I wonder what most Bauhaus members lived on. But the happiness and fullness of those years made us forget our poverty. Bauhaus members came from all social classes. They made a vivid appearance, some still in uniform, some barefoot or in sandals, some with the long beards of artists or ascetics. Some came from the youth movements.' [15]

In theory, therefore, Gropius had ideal material to work with—a new school, the opportunity of appointing a new staff, and enthusiastic students. In practice, however, it must have taken great courage and optimism, as well as sheer stamina, to keep alive his vision during those early years in Weimar. The vicious attacks from the Weimar establishment began almost immediately he took up his appointment; as soon, in fact, as the existing staff of the Academy of Fine Arts whom Gropius had inherited along with the school, realized that there was no place for them in the new régime. When he took over, the vacancies at the suspended school of arts and crafts enabled Gropius to make three new appointments, and he asked Lyonel Feininger, Johannes Itten and Gerhard Marcks to join him in Weimar. Marcks and Itten were comparatively unknown at that time, but by appointing Feininger Gropius stood condemned in the eyes of Weimar. For Feininger was an Expressionist, one of the revolutionaries who supported the alien and anarchistic ideas that had swept through Germany as soon as her frontiers were opened up again. (Gropius had, in fact, met him at meetings of the Novembergruppe.) His work was anathema to the bureaucracy and the 'academic' artists of Weimar, who felt his presence an insult to the former academy.

Bird cloud oil, Lyonel Feininger *Photograph courtesy Busch-Reisinger Museum*

Walther Scheidig, in *Crafts of the Weimar Bauhaus* [16], describes how these criticisms were first muted, since Gropius's opponents thought that his appointment and the decision to combine and rename the schools had the approval of the Grand Duke. Then Fritz Mackensen declared that the Duke had never given his offical blessing to such a move and von Fritsch, who had by then also retired, revealed that he had made the appointment without consulting the Duke. From then on Gropius's relations with the officials and citizens of Weimar deteriorated, and for the next five years he was to fight a series of frustrating and time-consuming battles, for more space, more money, and finally for the right to exist in Weimar.

He also had many battles, both economic and ideological, to fight within the Bauhaus. In 1919, when he took over, the school seemed financially sound ; money for use by the suspended school

Earthenware teapot with raffia covered handle, Theo Bogler, 1922–3

of arts and crafts had been accumulating throughout the war, and Gropius had also initiated a Bauhaus fund, which, between April and October 1919, had received nearly a million marks. But he needed all the money he could get at that time, not only to help his impoverished students, but to establish workshops, and with them the type of instruction he required—the combined training by two masters, one an artist, one a technician—which was to be the hallmark of the Weimar period.

The curriculum was based on 'practical' and 'formal' instruction. The practical work consisted of studies of materials and working processes, while the 'formal' instruction was divided into three parts: *Observation*: the study of nature and materials; *Representation*: the study of geometry, construction, draughtsmanship and model-making; and *Composition*: the study of volume,

Earthenware cocoa pot, Otto Lindig, 1923

colour and design. The apprentice had to pass through three courses; the first was the famous preliminary course, lasting six months, which was aimed at purging the student of all conventionally acquired knowledge in order to introduce him to workshop theory and practice. If he passed this course the student then went in to one of the workshops. Workshop instruction lasted three years, and culminated in a journeyman's diploma. Only journeymen who had this official trade diploma were qualified to take the culminating architectural course, and for this a Bauhaus Research Department was planned.

These were the ideals, but it was far from easy to put them into practice. When van de Velde's school was closed down most of the workshops were dismantled and after deflation, in 1921, it became extremely difficult to find the money to restock them. Gropius,

Tapestry with flying bird, attributed to Paul Klee, *c.* 1921

Opposite:
Tapestry by Hedwig Jungnick, 1921–2

writes Scheidig, 'was not given a chance to let his ideas mature . . . he had to spend his days fighting for money from the state, for working space for the school, places to live in for teachers and students, money and food for the Bauhaus kitchen'. Nevertheless he was slowly able to evolve a teaching programme, although progress was more rapid in some areas than in others. The weaving workshop was the first to become reasonably well established; Hélène Börner, who had worked with van de Velde, had remained at the school and she became the weaver's *Lehrmeister*—the technician, while in 1920 Georg Muche, a young painter, was appointed *Formmeister* in order to provide the artistic inspiration. Under this joint instruction, and with the help of other painter weavers such as Hedwig Jungnick, Benita Otte and, above all, Gunta Stölzl an original and distinctive style emerged. (Paul Klee, who had joined the Bauhaus early in 1920, also produced designs for the weavers.)

Haus Sommerfeld, Walter Gropius with Adolf Meyer, 1921

Opposite:
Festival programme for the Haus Sommerfeld, designer unknown, 1920

It was some time before a satisfactory pottery workshop could be set up, and Gropius had to go to Dornburg, a small town about twenty miles outside Weimar, in order to find the space and the facilities. Gerhard Marcks, who came to the Bauhaus at the same time as Itten and Feininger, was made *Formmeister*, and the owner of the Dornburg pottery, Max Krehan, was the *Lehrmeister*. Here, as in the weaving workshop, there was a steady flow of excellent work, for in Otto Lindig and Theo Bogler the workshop had exceptional apprentices.

Gropius himself ran the wood-working shop in the early period; in 1921 he received a private commission to build a house near Berlin for Adolf Sommerfeld, a timber merchant. This gave him the opportunity to provide some of his apprentices with paid work,

BERLIN 18·12·1920

RICHTFEST DES WOHNHAUSES

· ADOLF · SOMMERFELD ·

Begrüßung der Geladenen.

Kreisgang der Handwerker mit dem Richtkranz

Zeichen des Sprechers zum Anzünden der 7 Richtfeuer

Sprecher ruft

Ring Kreis Kranz

Vollender der Gegensätze

Anfang und Ende
Mann und Weib
Geist und Leib
Bewegung und Ruhe
Körper und Raum
Grundriß und Aufriß

Ring Kreis Kranz

Beginn und Vollendung
ewiger Arbeit
kreisender Arbeit
vereinter Arbeit

Zeichen des Bauens:

Ring Kreis Kranz

Polier spricht

and the Haus Sommerfeld became a sort of shrine to the woodworkers' craft. Everything in it was designed and made by Bauhaus students in a riot of styles and contemporary clichés. For Gropius tried from the beginning to pursue a policy of non-interference, giving staff and students alike the freedom to experiment and develop a personal approach. Soon after he joined the Bauhaus in 1919 Lyonel Feininger wrote to his wife: 'Gropius sees craft in art, and I see only spirit (*Geist*). But he would never ask me to modify my approach to art, and I will stand by him in every possible way because he is a genuine and sincere man, a great idealist, and totally without egoism.' [17]

Nevertheless Gropius's vision of a team of 'men who would work, not automatically as an orchestra who obeys its conductor's baton, but independently although in close cooperation to further a common cause' nearly broke down in those early years of the Bauhaus, and the cause of the greatest unrest was Johannes Itten, who paradoxically enough, ran the most 'progressive' course in those early years.

Itten, was born in Switzerland in 1888, and he began his career as an elementary school teacher (at the time when Froebel and Pestalozzi were pioneering their new ideals of 'learning through doing'). In 1912 Itten embarked on a renaissance-style pilgrimage of art schools and universities in Switzerland, Germany, Belgium, Holland and Austria, studying art, mathematics and natural sciences, and in 1915 he opened a private art school in Vienna. Alma Mahler, who was to be Gropius's first wife, also lived in Vienna at that time, and she introduced Itten to Gropius, who was impressed by his teaching methods. In 1919 Gropius asked him to the Bauhaus in order to run the *Vorkurs*, the six-months preliminary course which all students had to take before they went on to more specialized training in one of the workshops.

Itten arrived in Weimar in May 1919, with a number of disciples from Vienna and immediately began to establish his course, intensifying the methods he had used in his own school. In 1922 he described his aims in a catalogue he wrote for an exhibition

Cover for a Bauhaus album, Johannes Itten, 1922–3

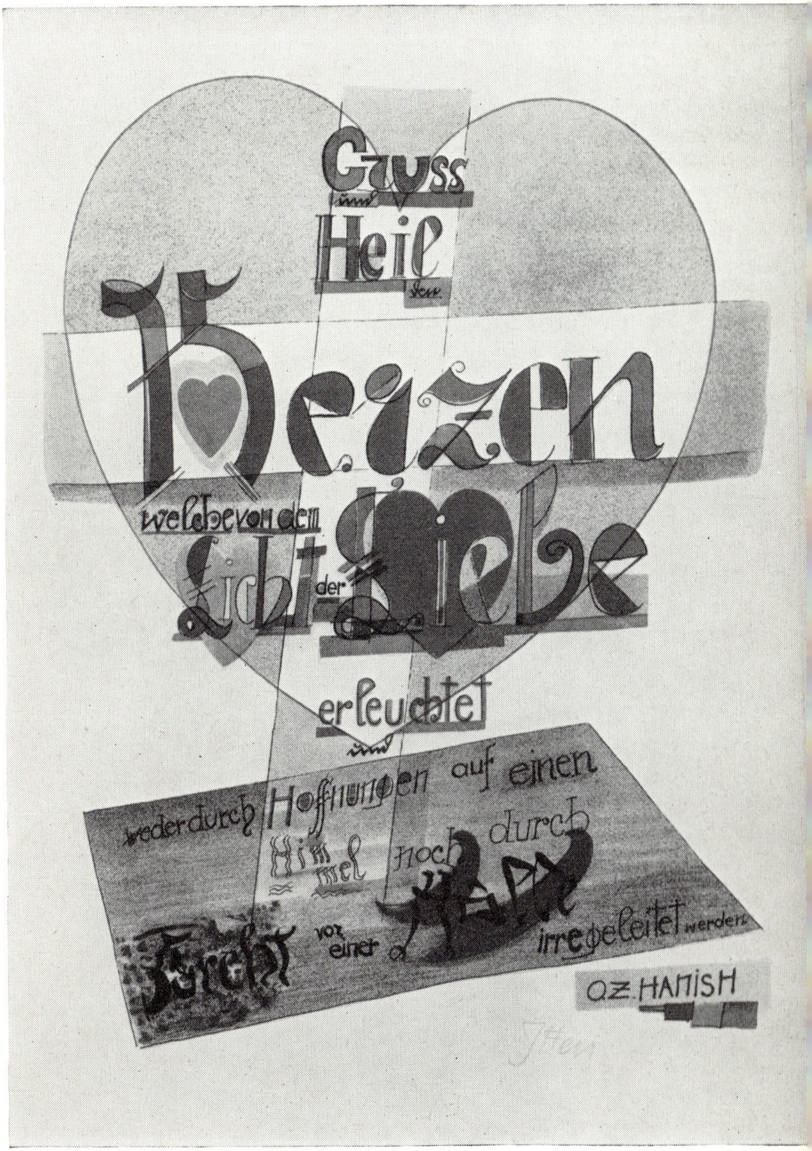
Gruss
und
Heil
den
Herzen
welche von dem
Licht der Liebe
erleuchtet
und
weder durch Hoffnungen auf einen
Himmel noch durch
Furcht vor einer
irregeleitet werden
O.Z. HANISH

of Bauhaus work: 'This course is intended to liberate the student's creative power, to give him an understanding of nature's materials, and to acquaint him with the basic principles which underlie all creative activity in the visual arts. Every new student arrives encumbered with a mass of accumulated information which he must abandon before he can achieve perception and knowledge that are really his own. If he is to work in wood, for example, he must know his material *thoroughly*, he must have a feeling for wood. He must also understand its relation to other materials, to stone, glass and wool. Consequently he works with these materials, as well, combining and composing them to make their relationships fully apparent.

'Preparatory work also involves exact depiction of actual materials. If a student draws or paints a piece of wood true to nature in every detail, it will help him to understand the material. The work of the old masters, such as Bosch, Master Francke or Grünewald also offers instruction in the study of form, which is an essential part of the preliminary course. This instruction is intended to enable the student to perceive the harmonious relationship of different rhythms and to express such harmony through the use of one or several materials. The preliminary course concerns the student's whole personality, since it seeks to liberate him, to make him stand on his own feet and it makes it possible for him to gain a knowledge of both material and form through direct experience.'[18]

Illustrations of students' work in the *Vorkurs* show how thoroughly Itten was able to put these ideals, the complete antithesis of traditional academic training techniques, into practice. In advocating direct experience and the designer's personal involvement with the materials he was to use, as well as the intensive study of the properties of these materials, Itten should, in theory, have produced students well equipped to develop and exploit the potential of the semi-craft techniques that were available in the Bauhaus workshops during the early years. In practice, however, his emphasis on an intuitive approach and the development of personality through the elimination of all previously acquired knowledge, together with his own personal brand of mysticism, led the students away from the realities that Gropius was attempting to instil, and set them off on a pursuit of the

Silver sauce jug with ebony handles Wilhelm Wagenfeld, 1924

Ashtray in bronze with tilting cigarette holder, Marianne Brandt, 1924

Teapot in bronze with ebony handles, Marianne Brandt, 1924

unconscious and a quest for inner harmony. Intuitive solutions were considered more valid than intellectual ones, and in order to develop their latent spiritual powers and induce trance-like states, suitable for meditation on shapes, sounds and colours, Itten's students were encouraged to sing, dance, act, eat special food, and do breathing exercises.

Itten had a tremendous influence on the half starved and war-shattered students in those early years. Helmut von Erffa who joined the Bauhaus in 1919 has described his impressions and experiences: 'We all hoped for a better life, and those hopes centred, not around Gropius at first, but around Johannes Itten. Gropius might share our simple meals in the Bauhaus canteen but it was Itten who was a leading spirit in those early days.'[19] His influence was, in fact, so strong that he and his followers began to decide who was worthy of the Bauhaus course. Even after they had been accepted by Gropius, prospective students had to be vetted by Itten's disciples. Von Erffa writes: 'After we had had an interview with Gropius we still had to be passed by a kind of one man student council. I remember my trepidation as I was led into the room, whitewashed and totally bare except for a huge black wooden cross on the wall. On a simple iron bedstead sat a haggard young man in a monk's habit. His cheeks were hollow, his eyes burned feverishly and he was one of Itten's most trusted pupils—"Really a saint," my companion whispered. He looked me over while my companion stood in respectful silence. Then he said something in an ecstatic singsong voice and nodded. He had seen none of my drawings and barely heard me utter a word, but I had passed the test and was accepted. "The master has complete trust in his intuitive judgment," my companion explained after we had left the room.'[20]

Obviously Itten's philosophy, with its stress on personal salvation through a mystic communion with matter, was totally alien to Gropius's aims for the school. While Gropius urged Bauhäusler to come to terms with reality, Itten's followers sought to transcend it, and in doing so they questioned the fundamental premises of Bauhaus teaching. They rejected the idea of workshop training, and the role of 'apprentice' and 'journeyman' was altogether too mundane for them, since they saw themselves as artists and individualists in whatever medium they chose to exploit. A

Coffee pot (*left*) by Wilhelm Wagenfeld; jug (*right*) by W. Rössger and Friedrich Marby, 1924

Gropius's room in the Weimar Bauhaus. Furniture designed by Gropius; light fittings, wallhanging and rug designed in the workshops

Electric table lamp, Wilhelm Wagenfeld, 1924

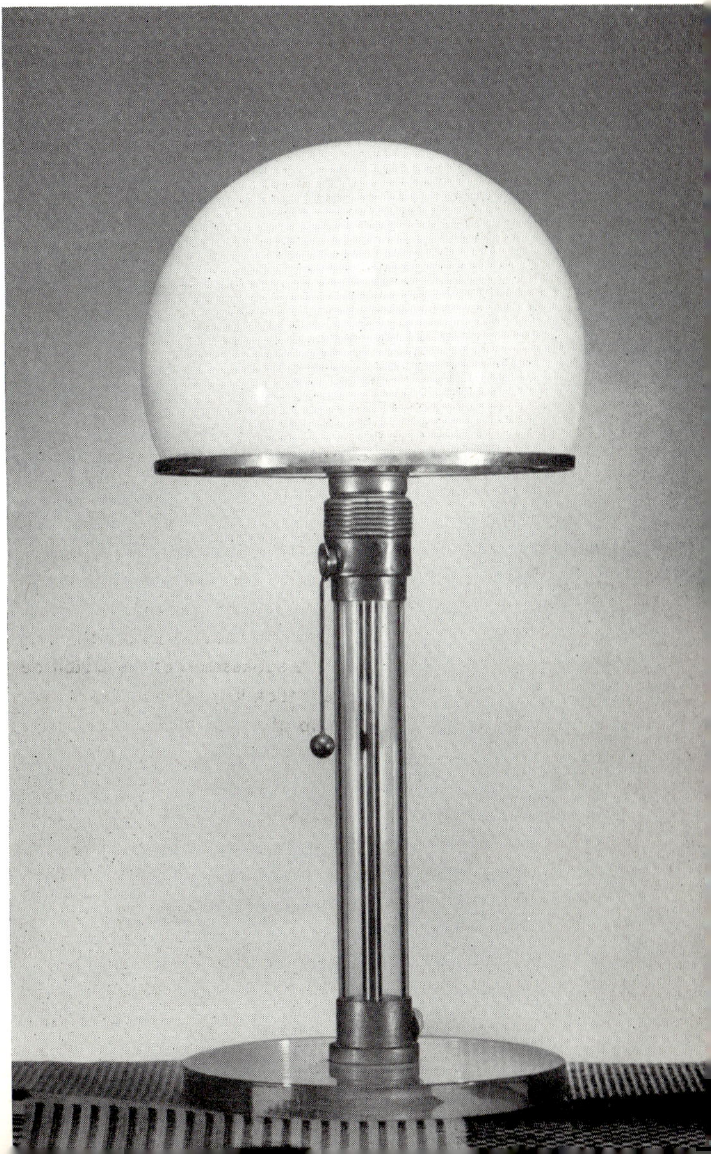

confrontation was inevitable, and with it the need to redefine the school's aims. In December 1921 and again in February 1922, Gropius addressed the staff (the texts are published for the first time in Wingler's *Das Bauhaus*) repeating his ideals of 1915 and 1919, and stressing the Bauhaus's commitments to society. 'Itten,' he wrote in 1922, 'has recently challenged us—we must each decide for ourselves whether we should pursue our individual talents in opposition to the outside world, or whether we should seek an affinity with industry . . . I am seeking for unity in the combination, not in the separation of these two ways of life.'

This crisis and clash of ideologies, however, laid bare the weaknesses in Bauhaus theory and practice at that time. Itten's mysticism was not far removed from the philosophy of the first manifesto: 'The artist is an exalted craftsman. In rare moments of inspiration, moments beyond this life, the grace of heaven may cause his work to blossom into art.' Gropius, however, had immediately qualified this by emphasizing (the passage is underlined in the original text) '*But proficiency in a craft is essential to every artist.*'

It was this practical approach, rather than its philosophical implications, that Gropius had to stress again and again when he was trying to reconcile the conflicting theories that were undermining the Bauhaus.

The 'hardening' of his attitude also coincided with the arrival in Weimar of Theo van Doesburg, the spokesman of the Dutch de Stijl group. The de Stijl movement took its name from a review, first published in 1917, by a group of Dutch painters, architects and sculptors, who, mainly inspired by the work of Mondrian, aimed at creating a style in painting, architecture and design that was rational, ordered, intellectual and completely impersonal. Van Doesburg, the most articulate member of this extremely articulate group, became its protaganist. He was 'convinced' that 'the moral worth of man will increase in a properly studied environment' [21] and that it was the responsibility of the architect, by means of objective scientific methods, to create and control this environment. An essay *Towards a Collective Construction* which he wrote for *De Stijl* in 1923, in collaboration with the architect and town planner, van Eesteren, defines the general attitude of the

Overleaf: Green-orange graduation with black half-moon, watercolour, Paul Klee, 1922
Photograph courtesy Busch-Reisinger Museum

group: 'We have to understand that art and life are no longer two separate domains. This is why the idea of "art" as an illusion separated from real life must disappear. The word "art" no longer means anything to us. Instead, therefore, we demand the construction of our surroundings according to creative laws, resulting from a stable principle. These laws, parallel to those of economy, mathematics, technique, hygiene, etc., will lead to a new plastic unity. In order to define the relation of these reciprocal laws, it becomes necessary to understand and to determine them. Until now the domain of human creation and its constructive laws have never been examined scientifically . . . One can only define them by collective work and by experience . . . Our epoch is hostile to every subjective speculation in art, science, technique, etc. The new spirit, which already governs almost all modern life, is opposed to animal spontaneity (lyricism), to nature's domination, to artistic flummery and cookery. In order to construct a new object we need a method, that is to say, an objective system. If one finds, in different objects, identical qualities, one has found an objective standard.' [22]

Van Doesburg had arrived in Weimar in 1921; in theory both de Stijl and the Bauhaus were pursuing similar aims—both were dedicated to the fusion of art and life and art and technology in order to create a more acceptable environment for twentieth-century man. But van Doesburg found the school dominated by Itten and devoted to obscure cults and self expression, 'the artistic flummery and cookery' he loathed. In 1922, therefore, he set up a rival course in Weimar which was well attended by Bauhaus students. Von Erffa has described the impact of his arrival. 'Theo van Doesburg burst upon us with a lecture on his group, while his wife played de Stijl music . . . As a champion of geometrical purity in architecture, van Doesburg must have thought us very provincial at first—I can still see his tall black-shirted figure monocling the students' collages with unconcealed horror.' Van Erffa goes on, 'De Stijl certainly had some influence on us, but even without van Doesburg's presence in Weimar, abstract art would have driven out Expressionism'. Van Doesburg himself, however, was convinced that he had weaned the Bauhaus from Expressionism to Constructivism. In 1929 he recalled: 'At the desire of many young artists, the author conceived in 1922

the plan of opening a Stijl course. This course, which has been mainly attended by pupils of the Bauhaus, contributed a great deal to reorientate the creative mentality, as just about that time the younger German artists turned away from the caprice of Expressionism. The intervention of de Stijl was extremely opportune for bringing the young artists into order and discipline.' [23]

Gropius, of course, with his obsession for impartiality and *laissez faire*, would never have attempted to bulldoze his young artists into order and discipline, but the presence in Weimar of van Doesburg, coupled with the negative influence of Itten, spurred him into reorganizing some of his courses and appointing new staff.

His decisions at that time were vital to the future of the Bauhaus. His revolutionary teaching programme was threatened by ideological and economic pressures, and his well defined aims for the school were being misinterpreted by students and staff, as well as by intelligent observers such as van Doesburg. The craft training which he saw as a means to an end was rapidly becoming an end in itself, with complete loss of contact with contemporary production problems. But in spite of this threatened disintegration of all his ideals for the school, Gropius refused to compromise on any fundamental issues. He was convinced that by bringing together artists and technicians he had the right formula for creating better standards in architecture and design, and, as always a diplomatist rather than a dictator, instead of dismissing Itten and tightening his own control, he made several changes in the administration of the workshops in order to confine Itten's influence to the preliminary course, where his unique methods could bring about positive results. Gropius then went on to reaffirm his belief in 'the common citizenship of all forms of creative work' by persuading Wassily Kandinsky to return from Russia in order to teach at the Bauhaus. Kandinsky's appointment was a triumph for Gropius, for this remote and intelligent artist, who had founded the *Blaue Reiter* group in 1911 and who, with his book *Concerning the Spiritual in Art*, published in 1912, had produced the first *credo*

Composition, watercolour, Wassily Kandinsky, 1922 *Photograph courtesy Busch-Reisinger Museum*

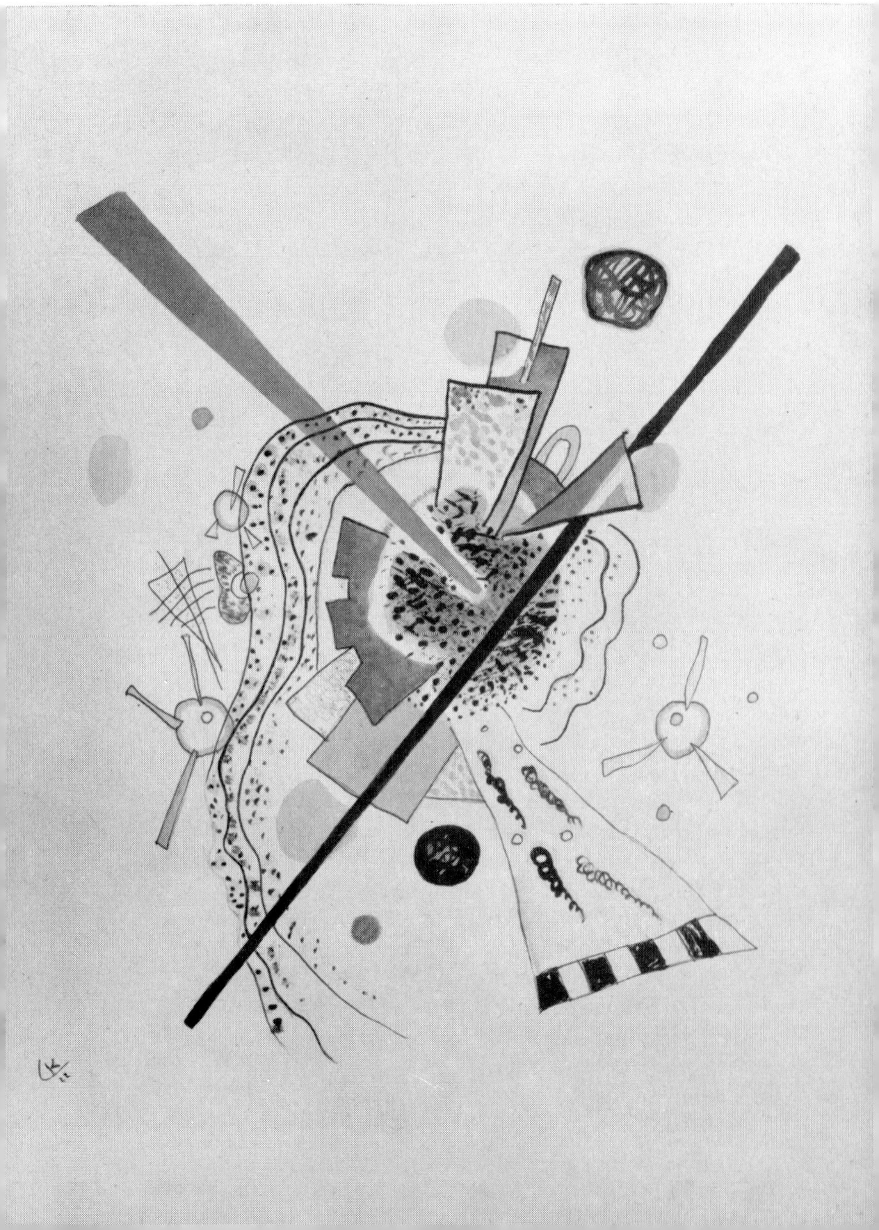

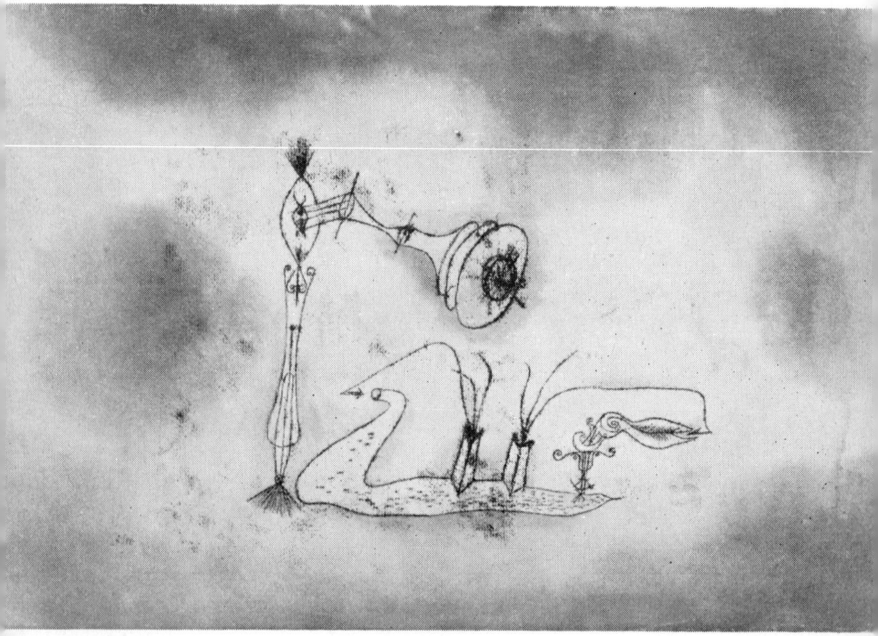

Magnetic apparatus for plant cultivation, watercolour, Paul Klee, 1921 *Photograph courtesy Busch-Reisinger Museum*

Opposite:
Composition 19 oil, L. Moholy-Nagy, 1920
Photograph courtesy Busch-Reisinger Museum

of the abstract artist, was one of the most powerful and influential painters of his generation. Gropius appointed him *Formmeister* in the department of mural decoration, and there with his analytical studies of form and colour, he did a great deal to counteract the iconoclasm of Itten. In Klee and Kandinsky Gropius had secured two painters of formidable intellect and originality, who aimed, in their theoretical courses, to teach their students how to use their eyes and brains in an entirely new way. They both attempted to analyse the fundamentals of artistic creation and to relate them to all levels of human experience, both conscious and unconscious. Their ideas were later reinforced and extended by Laszlo Moholy-Nagy, who joined the staff as a replacement for Itten when the latter left in 1923.

19
Moholy-Nagy

Moholy-Nagy was then twenty-eight years old; he was a Hungarian and had been working in Berlin since 1921 as editor of the *avant-garde* Hungarian art journal *MA*. There he met 'the Russian artists El Lissitzky, Ilya Ehrenburg and later Gabo . . . they brought news of Malevich, Rodchenko and the movement called Suprematism'.[24] He also met van Doesburg, and was sufficiently impressed by his ideas to attend the Constructivist conference he organized in Weimar in 1922.

By taking in someone from the 'enemy' camp, Gropius obviously hoped to gain some measure of support from the de Stijl group, but he also secured the cooperation of an enthusiastic and dedicated educationalist, whose preoccupations extended beyond the language of painting to typography, photography and the cinema.

In his preface to the 1947 edition of Moholy-Nagy's book *The New Vision* Gropius wrote: 'Moholy was one of my most active colleagues in building up the Bauhaus. Much that it accomplished stands to his credit.' Moholy was, in fact, quick to recognize the potential of the curriculum Gropius was attempting to establish, and he was sympathetic to the ideal of synthesis that the Bauhaus represented. He was also popular with the students; a generation younger than Klee and Kandinsky, an extrovert and an enthusiast, they could never accuse him of being a *'Korridor-Meister'*. (Oskar Schlemmer describes in his diary how some of the students complained that the 'artists' were at the Bauhaus for prestige purposes, and rarely appeared in the workshops, where the real work was being done.)

Gropius's conviction that something positive would emerge from the interaction of all these personalities was put to the test far earlier than he would have wished. In the summer of 1923 the Thuringian government stepped up its campaign against the Bauhaus by demanding a comprehensive exhibition. Although Gropius was reluctant to be forced into a demonstration of Bauhaus achievement only four years after it had been opened, there is no doubt that the exhibition proved to be a turning point in the

Light-space modulator, L. Moholy-Nagy, 1922–30
Photograph courtesy Busch-Reisinger Museum

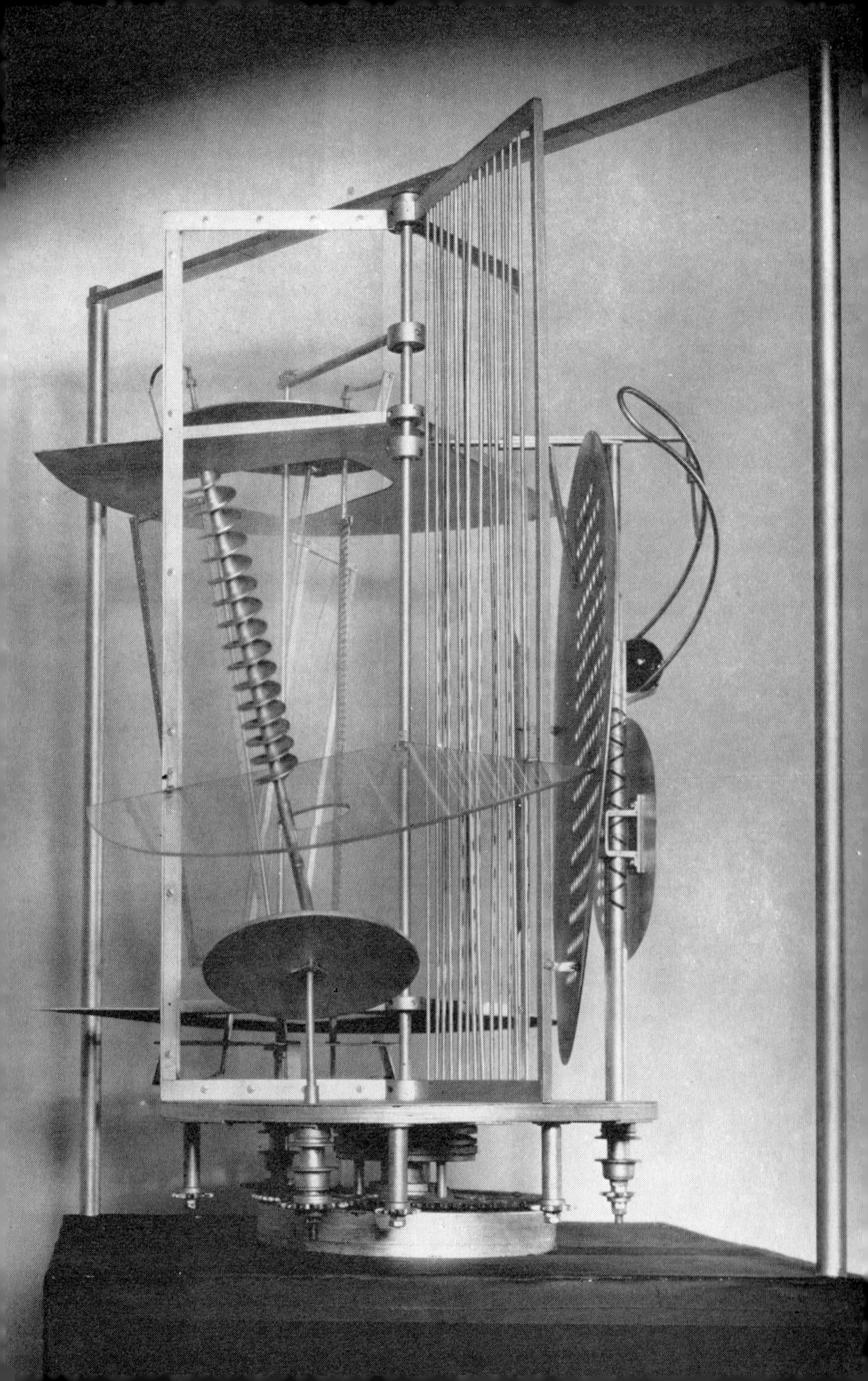

history of the school. By working together on a common project, students and staff at last seemed to realize why they were at the school, for out of the tentative experiments and philosophizing of the first four years a positive and self confident style had emerged. Although most of the workshops were using craft rather than machine techniques, several of the designs they produced could well have served as prototypes for industry; in fact, the pottery workshops, which were still based some miles out of Weimar, were able to show porcelain that was already in production. At the same time the staff grew more realistic. Schlemmer talks in his diaries of 'turning away from Utopia', and Lyonel Feininger wrote to his wife: 'So much is obvious . . . if we do not prove ourselves by "deeds" and win over the industrialists, we can forget our future hopes for the Bauhaus.'[25]

Opposite:
Easy chair in cherry with woven seat and backrest, Marcel Breuer, 1922

Low tea table in pear, Marcel Breuer, 1921–2

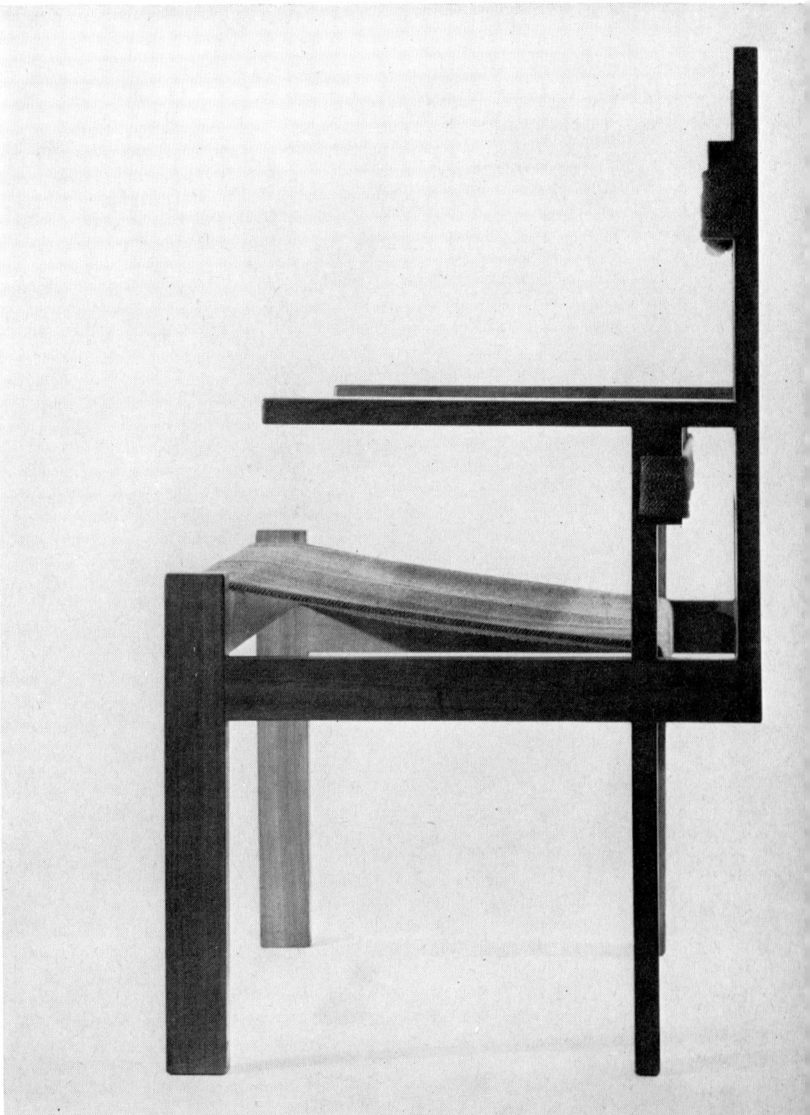

The most fundamental change of approach, however, was apparent in the carpentry workshop; here the most outstanding designer was Marcel Breuer, whom van Doesburg had described as one of the 'young artists he had brought to order and discipline'. Breuer had come to the Bauhaus as a student in 1920 (he was then eighteen); his main interest from the start was furniture and he had produced some solid Cubist-inspired designs for the Haus Sommerfeld in 1921. De Stijl Constructivism, with its emphasis on purity of form and structure, obviously had a great deal to offer,

Chair by Gerrit Rietveld, 1917

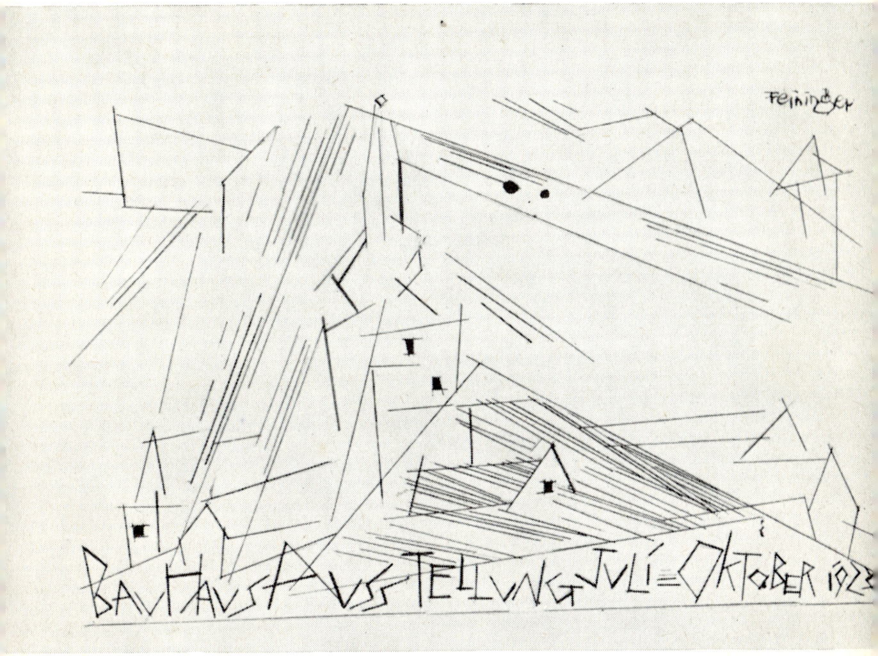

Design for a postcard announcing the Bauhaus Exhibition, 1923; woodcut, Lyonel Feininger *Photograph courtesy Busch-Reisinger Museum*

in those early years, to a designer such as Breuer, and Gerrit Rietveld's famous chair, first produced in 1917 and illustrated in *De Stijl* in 1922, was clearly the inspiration for the change of style in the carpentry workshops. Rietveld's chair is made from pieces of unbent plywood and wooden square members, each 'visibly connected', as Rietveld put it, with screws. The relationship between each member was carefully calculated so that the whole design had a geometrical precision, and similar principles govern the design of most of the furniture produced for the exhibition.

Jocular sounds oil, Wassily Kandinsky, 1929 *Photograph courtesy Busch-Reisinger Museum*

Opposite:
Perception of an animal ink, Paul Klee, 1925
Photograph courtesy Busch-Reisinger Museum

This took place in August and September 1923; work from every department was on display—in the workshops, the corridors, the halls and staircases; extra-mural work was shown in the *Staatliches Landesmuseum*. In fact Weimar, for those few weeks, was the focal point of the *avant garde* of Europe. There were exhibits by the 'Old Masters' . . . Klee, Kandinsky, Feininger and Schlemmer who had already made their reputation, and by the

Haus am Horn, Georg Muche and Adolf Meyer, 1923

Opposite:
White porcelain coffee pot, designed by Otto Lindig and made by Staatliche Manufaktur, Berlin, 1923

'new men'—Breuer, Josef Albers, Herbert Bayer and Moholy-Nagy, who were to train a new generation of designers, first at Dessau and finally in the United States. There were lectures by Gropius, Kandinsky and J. J. P. Oud, and concerts of new works by Stravinsky, Busoni and Hindemith. Oskar Schemmer's Triadic Ballet was also performed, demonstrating his theories on the relationship between human form and movement.

Pride of place in the exhibition, however, went to the *Versuch-haus am Horn*, an experimental house designed by Georg Muche and Adolf Meyer, which was furnished throughout with designs from the workshops. This house was originally planned as a

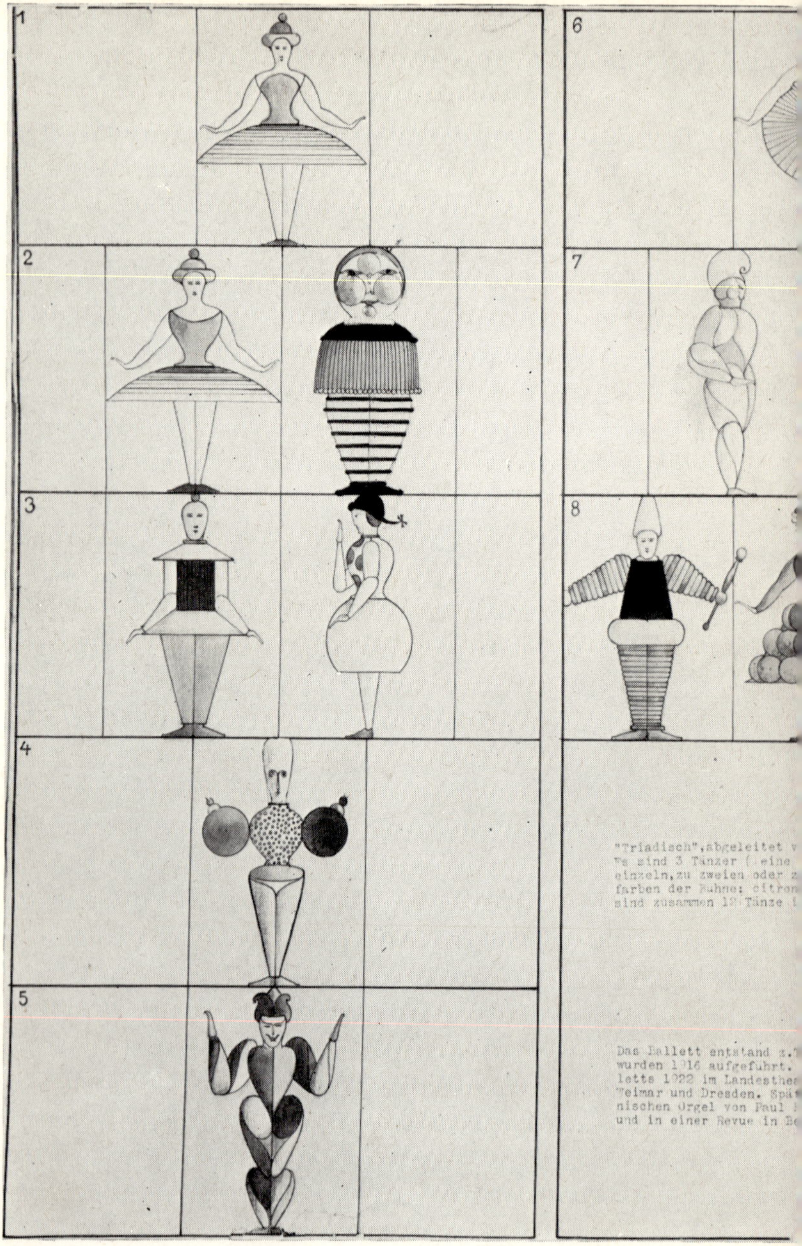

Costume studies for Triadic Ballet, Oskar Schlemmer, 1922 *Photograph courtesy Busch-Reisinger Museum*

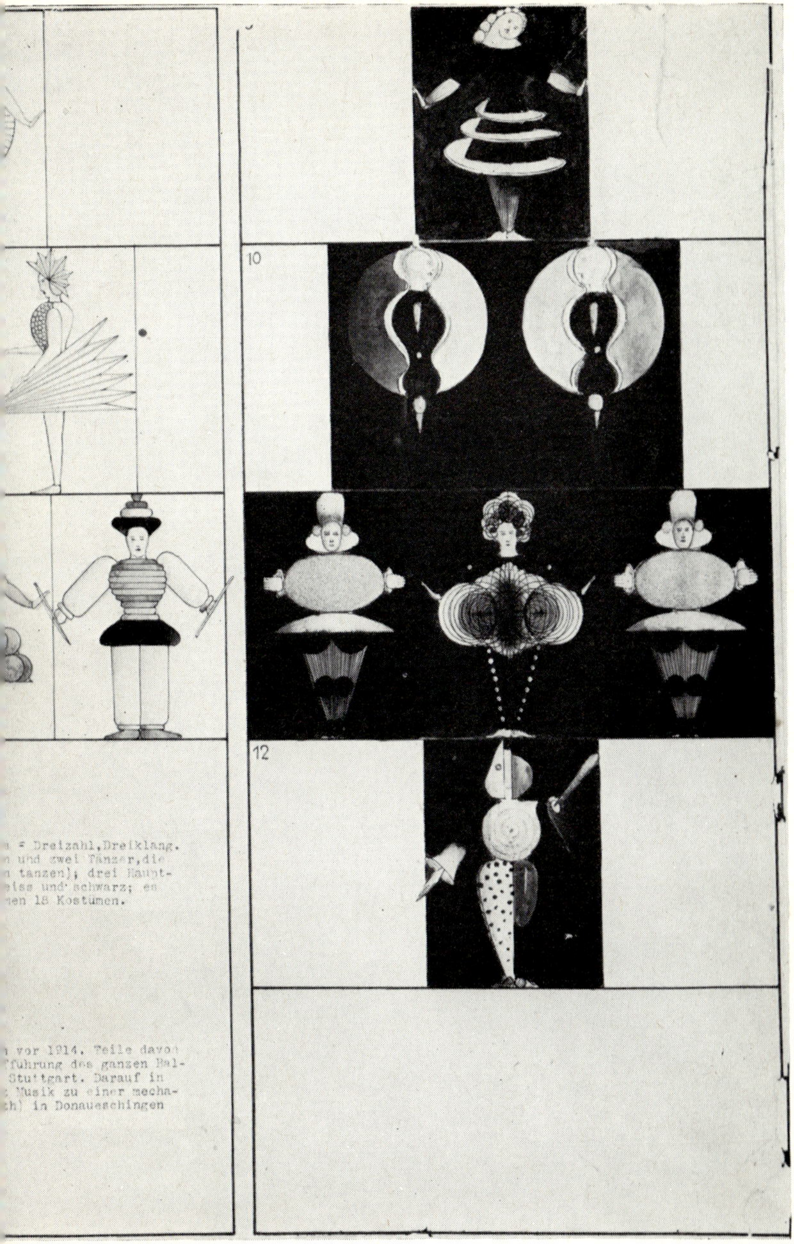
10
12
= Dreizahl,Dreiklang.
und zwei Tänzer,die
tanzen); drei Haupt-
eiss und schwarz; es
en 18 Kostümen.
vor 1914. Teile davo
führung des ganzen Bal-
Stuttgart. Darauf in
Musik zu einer mecha-
ch) in Donaueschingen

Opposite:
Chair in pear, Marcel Breuer; fabric designed by Gunta Stölzl, 1922–3

Nursery table and chairs, Marcel Breuer, 1923

Bauhaus settlement for students and staff that was to be built on the outskirts of Weimar; the scheme had to be abandoned, however, partly because of the uneasy position of the Bauhaus in Weimar, and partly because of the economic situation.

The house provided a practical demonstration of the style that had emerged from the fusion of the aesthetic and the workshop approach. The fact that the Bauhaus had finally found its sense of direction was further emphasized by the title of Gropius's lecture *Art and Technics: a new unity*, and by the publication that year of his *Idee und Aufbau des Staatlichen Bauhauses Weimar*. In this important essay Gropius defines his school's position in relation to the past academic training which turned out 'social drones, useless, by virtue of their schooling, in the productive life of the nation'; for the first time he gives a complete breakdown of the courses that were to lead up to the education of a new kind of architect; and finally, to combat the criticisms of those who queried the relevance of the Bauhaus stress on craft training, he again emphasized that mastery in a craft must be considered as a means to an end. 'The Bauhaus does not pretend to be a crafts school; contact with industry is consciously sought . . . the old craft workshops will develop into industrial laboratories: from their experimentation will evolve standards for industrial production . . . The teaching of a craft is meant to prepare for designing for mass production. Starting with the simplest tools and least complicated jobs, he gradually acquires ability to master more intricate problems and to work with machinery, while at the same time he keeps in touch with the entire process of production from start to finish.'

However, in spite of the success of the exhibition (it was visited by 15,000 people, and acclaimed by critics in Europe, America and Canada), it became increasingly obvious that the Weimar bureaucracy was determined to get rid of the Bauhaus. In the election of 1924, the conservatives had ousted the socialist majority, and under the new political régime the Bauhaus was accused of subversion and Bolshevism. It was even subject to police raids. In order to gain time, Gropius did his best to find some compromise

Secretaire in cherry and plum, Bengt von Rosen, 1923–4

Book jacket for Gropius's *Idee und Aufbau des Staatlichen Bauhauses Weimar*
L. Moholy-Nagy, 1923

Opposite:
Bank notes, Herbert Bayer, 1923

1000000
EINE MILLION MARK
WEIMAR, DEN 9. AUGUST 1923
DIE LANDESREGIERUNG
1000000 Mark zahlt die Kasse der Thüringischen Staatsbank dem Einlieferer dieses Notgeldscheines. – Vom 1. September 1923 ab kann dieses Notgeld aufgerufen und gegen Umtausch in Reichsbanknoten eingezogen werden.
Wer Banknoten nachmacht oder verfälscht oder nachgemachte oder verfälschte sich verschafft und in den Verkehr bringt, wird mit Zuchthaus nicht unter zwei Jahren bestraft.
Ungültig
2000000
ZWEI MILLION MARK
2000000 Mark zahlt die Kasse der Thüringischen Staatsbank dem Einlieferer dieses Notgeldscheines. – Vom 1. September 1923 ab kann dieses Notgeld aufgerufen und gegen Umtausch in Reichsbanknoten eingezogen werden.

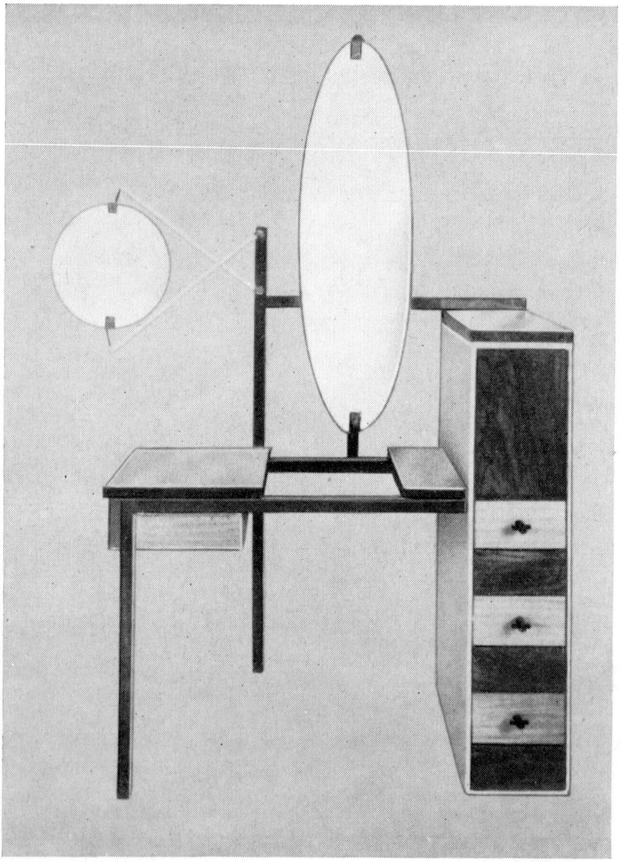

Dressing table, Marcel Breuer, 1923

solution, and suggested that the workshops should gear themselves for full-scale commercial production in order to secure some measure of financial independence for the school. These efforts, however, met with little success; in September 1924, the Thuringian Ministry gave 'cautionary' notice to all the staff, and on 23 December that year they declared that the Bauhaus could only continue if new contracts were signed, giving the government

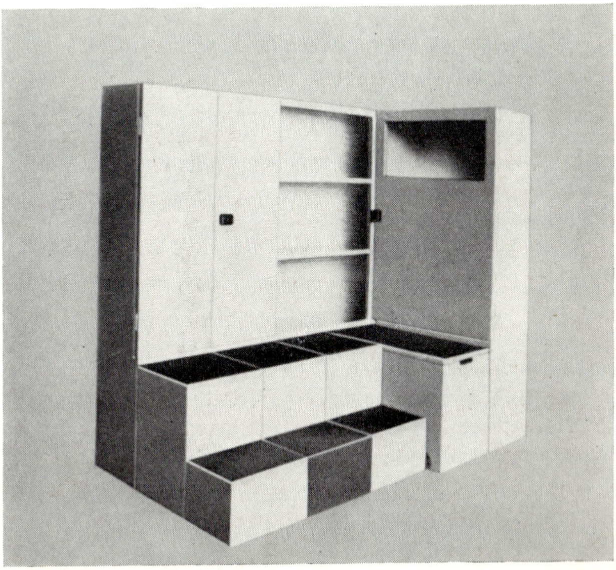

Dressing table, Alma Buscher, 1924

powers to dismiss the staff with six months' notice. This had the desired effect, and three days later Gropius sent the following letter to the Government of Thuringia: 'The Directors and masters of the State Bauhaus at Weimar, compelled by the attitude of the Government of Thuringia, herewith announce their decision to close the institution created by them on their own initiative and according to their convictions, on the expiration date of their contracts, that is April 1st, nineteen hundred and twenty-five. We accuse the Government of Thuringia of having permitted and approved the frustration of culturally important and always non-political efforts through the intrigues of hostile political parties . . .'

This letter was signed by Gropius and all the staff and it was followed by one from the students: 'We notify the Government of Thuringia that we, collaborators at the State Bauhaus Weimar, shall leave the Bauhaus, together with the leaders of the Bauhaus, because of the actions of the State Government . . .'

The threatened extinction of the Bauhaus aroused a storm of protest; eminent architects and artists wrote to the government; newspapers and magazines attacked their parochial decision and even van Doesburg rallied to the school's defence. 'Where else but here in Weimar was a generation, struggling for self-expression, offered the possibility of developing its creative powers? Neither in France, nor in England nor anywhere else was there an institution where the students themselves were encouraged to create, instead of being taught merely to repeat what had already been created. The Bauhaus is open to criticism in many respects; as a whole it shall not and must not be attacked.'

In the face of this storm, Bauhaus staff and students put on a united front; many of the staff were offered posts in other art schools but they refused these offers, and waited to see if the Bauhaus might be re-established in another city. Several town councils, including those of Darmstadt, Frankfurt and Mannheim, expressed interest in this idea, but Gropius entered into negotiations with Dr Fritz Hesse, the mayor of Dessau, then a small but expanding town, with flourishing local industries. On 1 April 1925, the Bauhaus moved with what equipment it possessed to Dessau; the workshops were set up in a local factory; lectures and seminars were held in the school of arts and crafts, and studios were established in the museum, and under these far from ideal conditions, Gropius began to reorganize the school.

The Bauhaus at Dessau, 1925–26 *Photograph courtesy Faber and Faber*

Dessau

From 1925 until Gropius left the school in 1929, the Bauhaus was building on the foundations that had been laid down in Weimar. The ideals and methods that had been so painfully evolved there were now generally accepted by students and staff, who, freed from bureaucratic pressures, were able to concentrate on Gropius's ideal of 'creating type forms that would meet all technical, aesthetic and commercial demands'. To mark this break with the past, and the spiritual 'coming of age' of the Bauhaus, Gropius altered the curriculum; the most significant change was the abolition of the dual system of workshop instruction, but Gropius was also able to extend the scope of the courses and establish a flexible method of instruction that allowed the staff to extend and develop their individual talents.

The *Vorkurs*, for example, was run jointly by Moholy-Nagy and Josef Albers, who each took a six months' course. Albers had been at the Bauhaus since 1923; in Weimar he had worked in the stained glass department, and he had also worked out his

own preliminary course, involving the study of materials, which for a time ran concurrently with Itten's. In Dessau he and Moholy concentrated, in their explorations of shapes, materials and structures, on their own particular preoccupations. Albers was primarily concerned with the basic elements of design, with what he called the 'structure, fracture and texture' of materials, while Moholy and his students explored spatial design, which at that time he defined as the 'interweaving of shapes; shapes which are ordered into certain well defined, if invisible, space relationships; shapes which represent the fluctuating play of tensions and forces'. At the same time Moholy and Albers were both involved in the work of other departments; Moholy remained in charge of the metal workshop, which he had taken over from Itten in 1935, and he was later to establish a course on photography. Both he and Albers were closely involved in the new print workshop which was set up under the direction of Herbert Bayer.

Bayer was one of five 'first generation' Bauhaus students who were asked to run new workshops. Marcel Breuer took charge of the furniture workshop. Joost Schmidt, who in Weimar had specialized in sculpture and had later become interested in typography, was put in charge of what was now called the 'plastic' workshop (Werkstatt für Plastik) where students took a basic course in the study of shape, form and volume; he also ran a course in visual design, in conjunction with the print workshop. Gunta Stölzl and Georg Muche were jointly responsible for the weaving department and Hinnerk Scheper, who had studied mural design in Weimar, was put in charge of the mural workshop. Klee and Kandinsky also ran compulsory courses, Kandinsky concentrating on analytical drawing, while Klee continued his

The Bauhaus workshop wing *Photograph courtesy Faber and Faber* intensive and wide ranging studies of form, space, movement and perspective. Feininger moved to Dessau, but did not teach there; he remained part of the community, however, and lived in one of the staff houses. Funds were not available to establish a pottery workshop in Dessau, so Gerhard Marcks left the school in 1925. Oskar Schlemmer ran the stage workshop as he had done in Weimar, and he was closely involved in the design of the experimental theatre at Dessau.

The Dessau era, therefore, opened with a period of intense activity for both students and staff, and their immediate task was to collaborate in the planning and furnishing of several buildings which the Dessau town council had commissioned from Gropius—the Bauhaus itself (comprising workshops, lecture rooms and students' quarters), a new building for the existing Dessau Arts and Crafts school, a housing colony, and a labour exchange. 'For their construction and equipment', writes Gropius, 'I brought the whole body of teachers and students into active cooperation. The acid test of attempting to co-ordinate several different branches of design in the actual course of building proved entirely successful . . . the band of fellow workers inspired by a common will I had once dreamed of had now become a reality.' [26]

Apart from the redesign of the State Theatre at Jena, completed for the opening of the Bauhaus exhibition of 1923, and the early work at Weimar—the uncharacteristic Haus Sommerfeld, and a war memorial for the town—Gropius and his partner Adolf Meyer had not been involved in any major architectural commissions since the Fagus factory and the Werkbund factory of the pre-Bauhaus era. Gropius had, however, maintained his reputation as an innovator and pioneer with his designs for the Chicago

The students' hostel, Bauhaus
Photograph courtesy Faber and Faber

Gropius's house, Dessau, 1926 *Photograph courtesy Faber and Faber*

Lecture theatre in the Bauhaus

Semi-detached houses for the Bauhaus staff, 1926 *Photograph courtesy Faber and Faber*

Tribune Tower competition of 1922, and with plans for an international academy of philosophical studies for the University of Erlangen (1924).

Neither of these projects was built, and the Bauhaus buildings at Dessau became Gropius's architectural manifesto, a visible expression of all the Bauhaus stood for. For this complex of buildings represented the fusion of technical, social and aesthetic requirements that Gropius had always aimed at. The school consisted of three main wings—the Dessau school of arts and crafts, the workshop block and the students' hostel. The arts and crafts school, a self-contained three-storey block, was united by means of a bridge across a roadway to the Bauhaus workshops. The bridge housed administrative rooms, clubrooms and Gropius's studio; the workshop wing, the largest in the whole complex, was three storeys high, with a printing shop and dye works in the basement; it was faced by a glass screen, and, as in the Fagus works, the supports were set well back so that the whole structure seemed to float in space. Another bridge, raised on piers, linked the workshop block with a students' hostel, a six storey building with twenty-eight student rooms each designed as a studio/bedroom and each with balcony. The bridging section contained a dining hall, auditorium, and a stage, and led into the foyer of the students' quarters. The walls surrounding the stage were removable, so that if necessary the dining room, stage, auditorium and vestibules could be opened up to form a large hall. Seven houses for Bauhaus staff were built in the grounds, and the Dessau Bauhaus was officially opened in December 1926.

For the first year at Dessau, therefore, most of the workshops were involved in work for the new buildings; tubular steel furniture for the assembly hall, dining room and students' rooms was designed by Marcel Breuer; all the light fittings were designed in the metal workshop and the wall-painting department was responsible for the interior decoration of the buildings.

During the transition period between the Bauhaus exhibition of 1923 and the opening of the new buildings in 1926, the workshops had established a characteristic style, both in product design and typography, that was to influence development in both these fields for the next fifty years. Gropius himself denied the existence of a 'Bauhaus' style, and argued that the acceptance

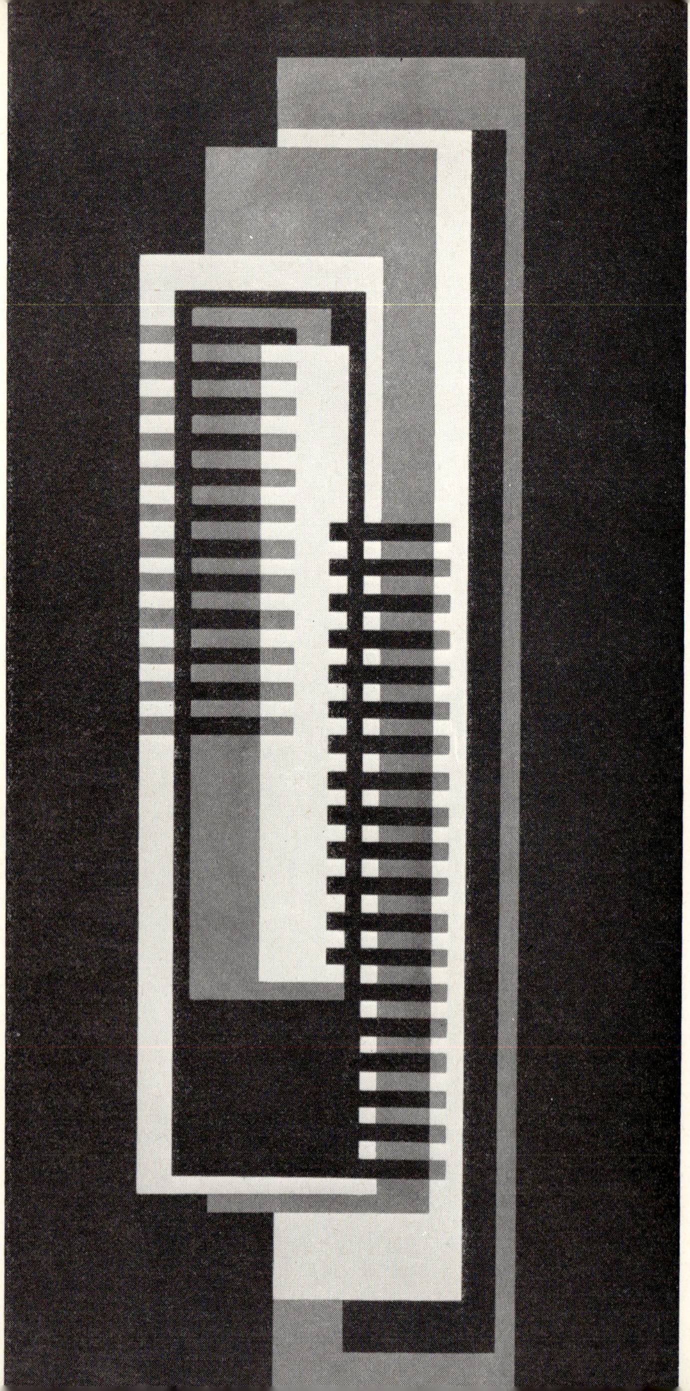

of preconceived ideas of form, even those developed within the Bauhaus, would have been 'a confession of failure and a return to that very stagnation and devitalized inertia which I had called it into being to combat'.[27] Nevertheless it was inevitable that a group of people working together in an experimental environment would tend to use the same sort of materials in the same sort of way, and that such dominant personalities as Moholy-Nagy, Marcel Breuer and Herbert Bayer, who were directly involved in the workshops, should communicate their personal vision to their students.

At Weimar, and in the early years at Dessau, this was essentially an artist's vision; for a brief period the theories of the Expressionists, then those of the Constructivists, influenced the choice of forms and materials for product design. (The pottery workshop, as has already been pointed out, was to a certain extent immune from these influences, and perhaps because of this was the first to establish links with industry.)

Van Doesburg introduced the Constructivist vision to Weimar, but it was above all Moholy-Nagy's personal interpretation of Constructivist attitudes that contributed to the emergence of a recognizable Bauhaus style. Moholy, who believed that 'mathematically harmonious shapes, executed precisely, are filled with emotional quality and represent the perfect balance between feeling and intellect',[28] was fascinated by the interplay of light and space, positive and negative, colour, transparency and the juxtaposition of textures. In *Abstract of an Artist* he described his preoccupations in 1919, before he came to the Bauhaus: 'On my walks I found scrap metal parts, screws, bolts, mechanical devices. I fastened, glued and nailed them on wooden boards, combined with drawings and paintings. It seemed to me in this way I would produce real spatial articulation, frontally and in profile, as well as more intense colour effects . . . I planned three-dimensional assemblages, constructions executed in glass and metal. Flooded with light I thought they would bring to the fore

Overlapping sandblasted laminated glass, Josef Albers, 1929

the most powerful of colour harmonies. In trying to sketch this type of "glass architecture" I hit upon the idea of transparency. This problem has occupied me for a long time.'

He brought these preoccupations to the Bauhaus, where he was put in charge of the metal workshop, and significantly enough he persuaded Gropius to allow the students there to work with glass as well as metal. This was the starting point for a whole series of experiments that were to revolutionize the light fittings industry, but there were several years of trial and error before the students' 'constructions' in glass and metal could serve as prototypes for industry.

Wilhelm Wagenfeld, a student in the metal workshop in Weimar, who was later to become well known as design consultant to the Jena glass works, has described how Moholy's paintings and abstractions in glass and metal were a direct inspiration for his famous table lamp of 1924 (see page 69).[29] He took great pains, in designing the lamp, to ensure a harmonious relationship between the various components and finishes (matt base, highly polished shaft and opal glass shade). Gropius and Moholy were both impressed by his prototype and decided that the lamp was suitable to offer to industry. So, in the primitive workshop which at that time, according to Wagenfeld, only possessed one ancient polishing machine, a series of Bauhaus lamps were made for exhibition at the Leipzig Fair of 1924. 'But,' wrote Wagenfeld, 'without success. Retailers and manufacturers

Composition A18 oil, L. Moholy-Nagy, 1927
Photograph courtesy Busch-Reisinger Museum

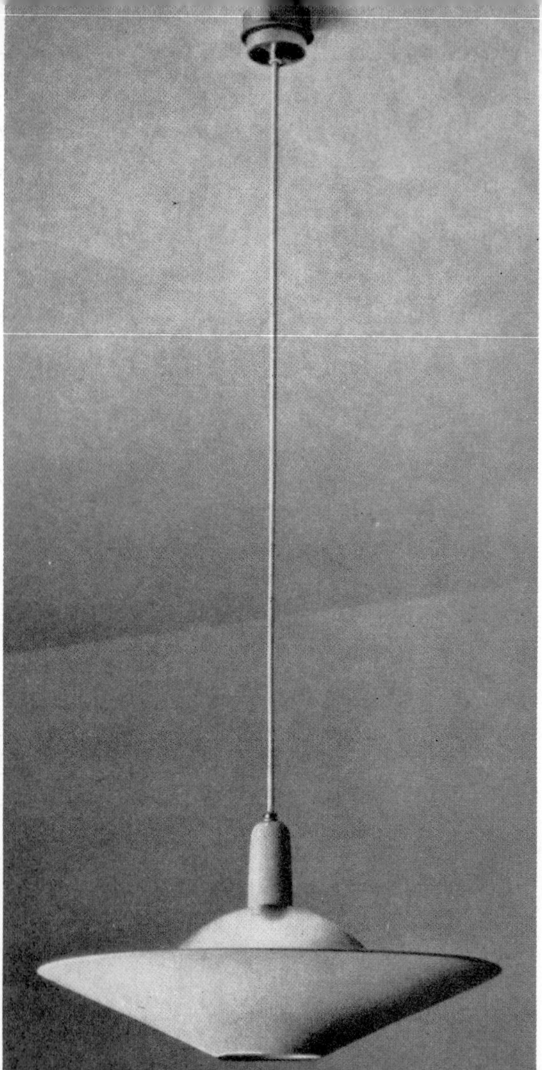

Ceiling light, Wilhelm Wagenfeld, 1927

laughed at our efforts. These designs which looked as though they could be made inexpensively by machine techniques, were, in fact, extremely costly craft designs.' It was very much later, according to Wagenfeld, that he realized that his lamp was a 'crippled, bloodless picture in glass and metal'.

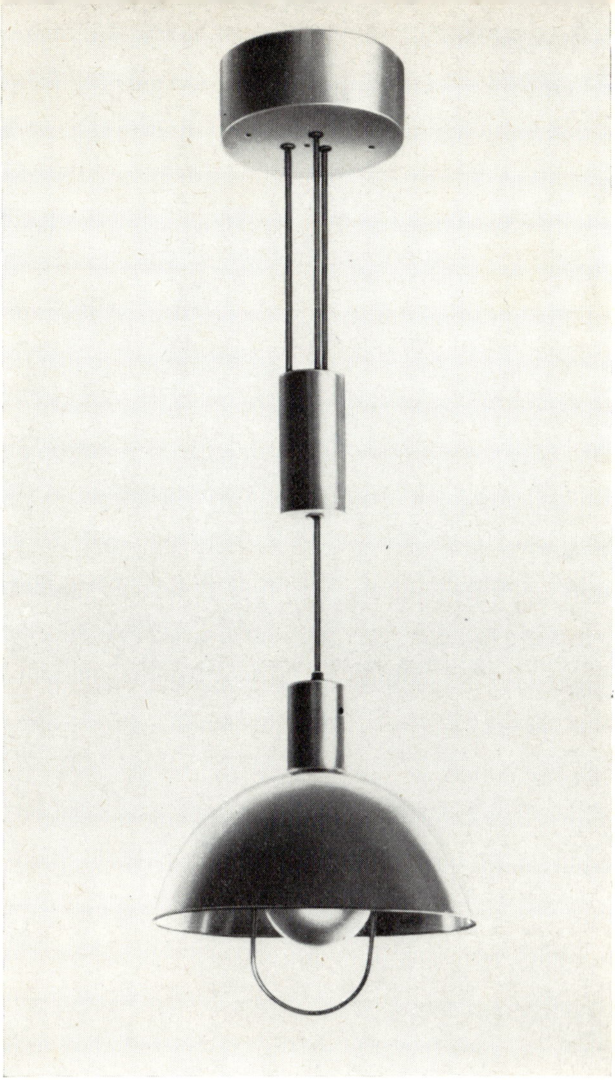

Ceiling light, Marianne Brandt, 1926

The transition from three-dimensional pictures to product design came at Dessau, where the workshops were adequately equipped and where there was much more active liaison with industry. It was here, in cooperation with outstanding students, such as Marianne Brandt, that Moholy's workshops were able to carry out genuine innovations, working with new materials and new combinations of materials to achieve functional solutions. 'I remember,' wrote Moholy 'the first lighting fixture by K. Jucker, done before 1923, with devices for pushing and pulling heavy strips and rods of iron and brass, looking more like a dinosaur than a functional object. But even this was a great victory, for it meant a new beginning. After this we developed lighting fixtures introducing such useful ideas as: the close fitting ceiling cap; combinations of opaque and frosted glass in simple forms technically determined by the action of the light; securing the globe to the metal chassis; the use of aluminium, particularly for reflectors.' [30] In fact, in the mid-'twenties, the Bauhaus metal workshop anticipated most subsequent developments in light fitting design, in both Europe and America, and ubiquitous design solutions that we now take for granted, were originated there.

A similar technical and aesthetic breakthrough was achieved by the carpentry workshop, which was renamed the furniture workshop after the move to Dessau. The change in title is significant, for early in 1925 Marcel Breuer had been investigating the possibility of using tubular steel for furniture, and his first design using that material was introduced later that year (it is still in production). He allegedly got the idea of using metal for furniture while admiring the curve of his handle bars as he cycled round Dessau, and once he had persuaded a manufacturer to let him have some of the material, he collaborated with a locksmith to produce a whole series of designs for chairs, tables and stools using the steel in combination with fabrics, glass and wood. By this use of metal he achieved the structural lightness, resilience and anonymity he had aimed at in wood, and whereas his Rietveld-inspired designs of Weimar have a certain static quality (less so, perhaps, than the original, since both the seat and the back rest are in canvas) his metal furniture is taut, light, almost transparent, in keeping with his belief that furniture should be 'drawn in space'.

From 1925 until he left the school in 1928, Breuer produced a whole series of designs using tubular steel, many of which were later mass produced by Standard-Möbel, a firm in Berlin, and by Thonet, by then well known for their designs in bentwood. His famous cantilever chair, however, was not designed until 1928,

First chair using tubular steel, Marcel Breuer, 1925

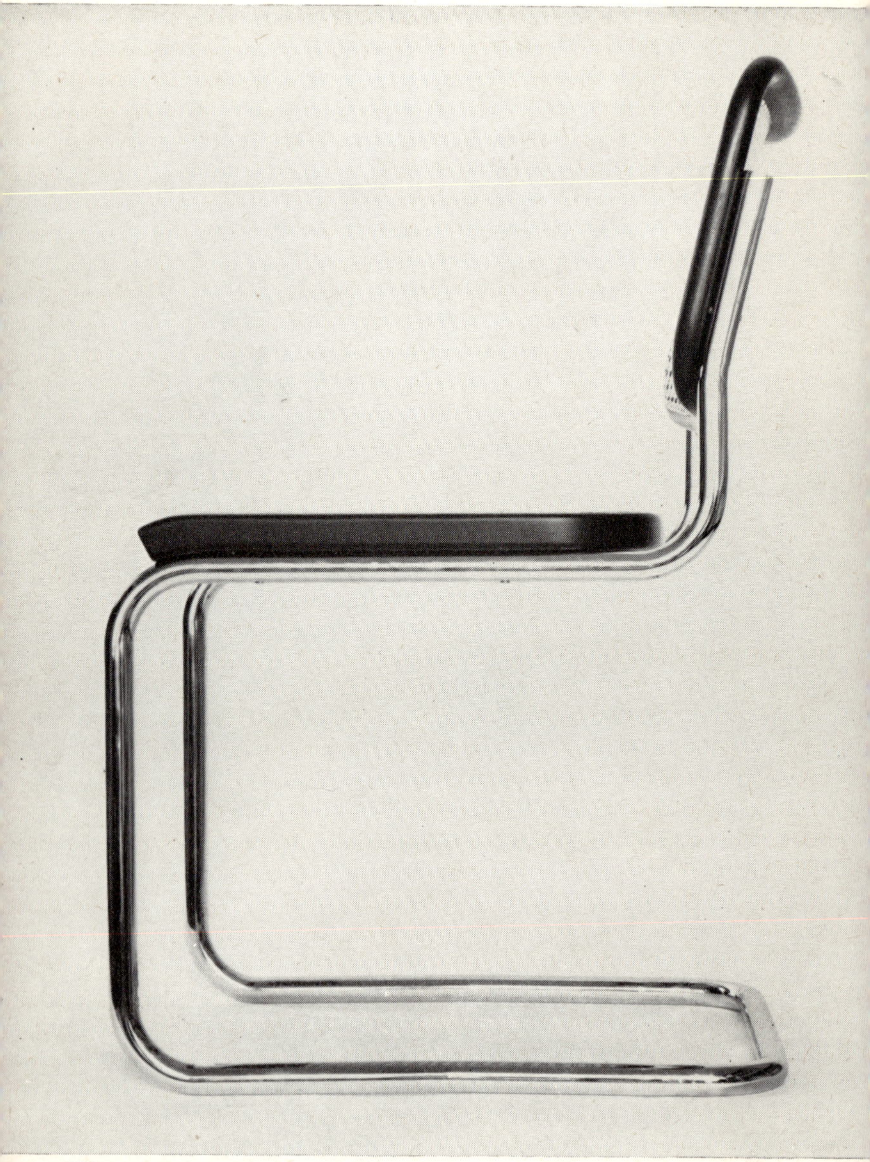

the year that he left the Bauhaus, and by that time several other architect/designers, including Mart Stam and Mies van der Rohe, had been experimenting with the material, and both had exhibited cantilever designs at the Werkbund Weissenhof settlement exhibition of 1927. Breuer's chair, however, has been prototype for the many thousands of 'S' chairs that have been subsequently mass produced the world over.

Opposite:
Breuer's cantilever chair, 1928

Cantilever chairs by Mies van der Rohe, 1928

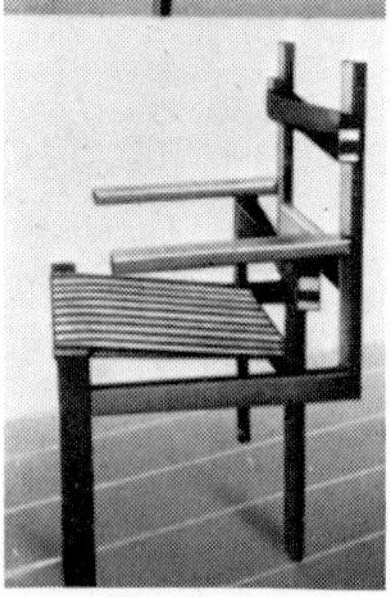

'Better and better every day.' Breuer's developments in chair design—'in the end we shall sit on resilient cushions of air'

Interior, with cantilever chairs, Mart Stam, 1928

As well as pioneering this revolution in seating design, Breuer was also preoccupied with the problem of standardization in furniture, and while he was at the Bauhaus he produced a scheme for a modular unit storage system, and designed built-in furniture for various apartments, including Gropius's house in Dessau. His underlying aim was to provide de-personalized furniture that could be used in any setting 'as would any living object like a flower or a human being'. 'A piece of furniture,' he wrote, 'is not

Standard furniture, made for the Feder Store, Berlin; Walter Gropius, 1927
Photograph courtesy Walter Gropius

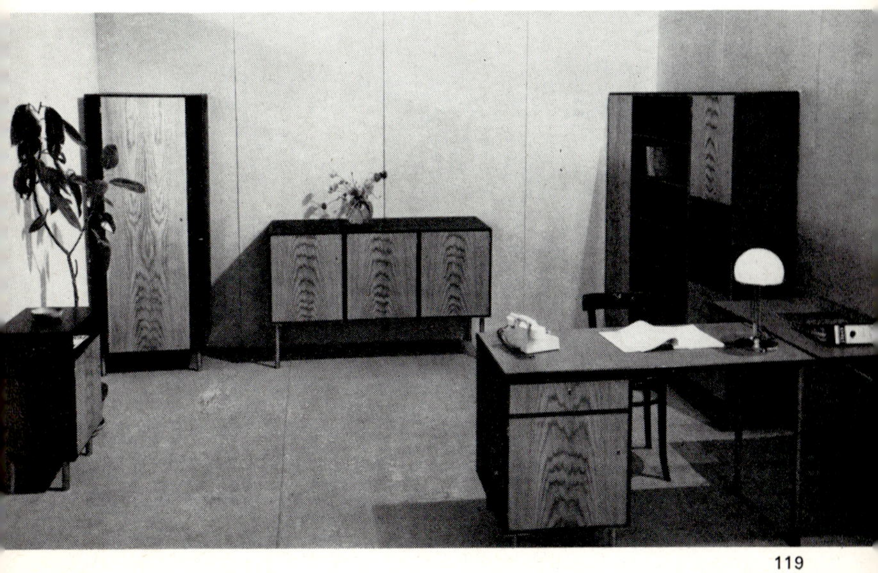

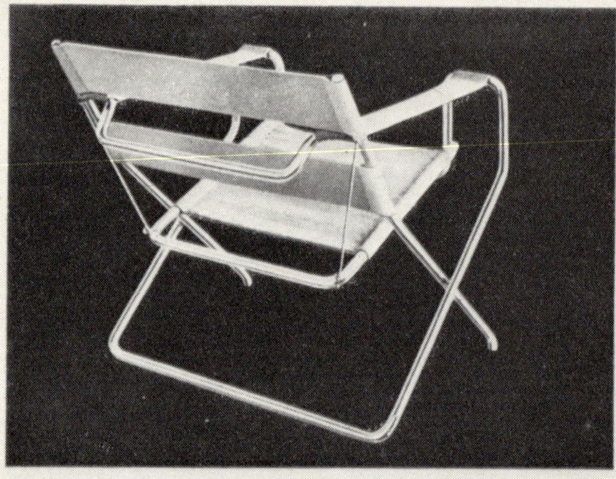

BREUER-METALLMÖBEL

HOCKER, STÜHLE, DREHSTÜHLE, KLUBSESSEL,
THEATERSESSEL, KLAPPSTÜHLE, TISCHE USW

die stoffbespannten stahlrohrmöbel haben die **bequemlichkeit** von guten polstermöbeln, ohne deren gewicht, preis, unhandlichkeit und unhygienische beschaffenheit. je ein **typ** wurde für die notwendigen anwendungsarten ausgearbeitet und soweit verbessert, bis eine variation nicht mehr möglich war. hier ist zum ersten mal präzisionsstahlrohr zur konstruktion von sitzmöbeln verwendet worden. das stahlrohr ist in geringen querschnittdimensionen widerstandsfähiger als irgend ein anderes material, welches bisher für sitzmöbel angewandt wurde. es ergibt besondere **leichtigkeit** und auch eine besonders leichte erscheinung. sämtliche typen sind **zerlegbar**. die teile sind auswechselbar. beim transport spielt die leichtigkeit eine große rolle. ein stahlklubsessel z. b. wiegt ca. 6 kg (ein viertel bis ein sechstel eines gepolsterten klubsessels). in teile zerlegt lassen sich ca. 54 klubsessel oder ca. 100 rückenlehnstühle in 1 cbm verpacken. der **preis** eines klubsessels z. b. beträgt ca. 30 prozent von dem eines gepolsterten sessels. der eines theatersessels oder eines rückenlehnstuhles, beide mit stoffbespannung, beträgt ca. 75 prozent vom preise ähnlich flachgepolsterter holzmöbel. durch ihre haltbarkeit und hygienische beschaffenheit sind die **breuer-metallmöbel** im gebrauch ca. 200 proz. wirtschaftlicher als die üblichen sitzmöbel.

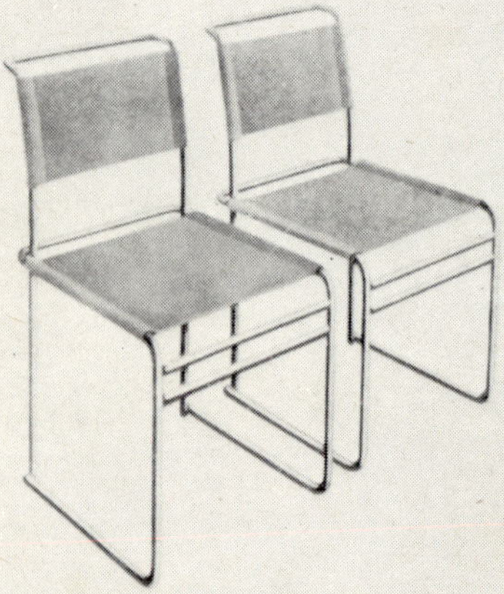

PRODUKTION UND VERTRIEB:

STANDARD-MÖBEL

LENGYEL & CO.

BERLIN W 62

Tel. Nollendorf 4009 BURGGRAFENSTRASSE 5

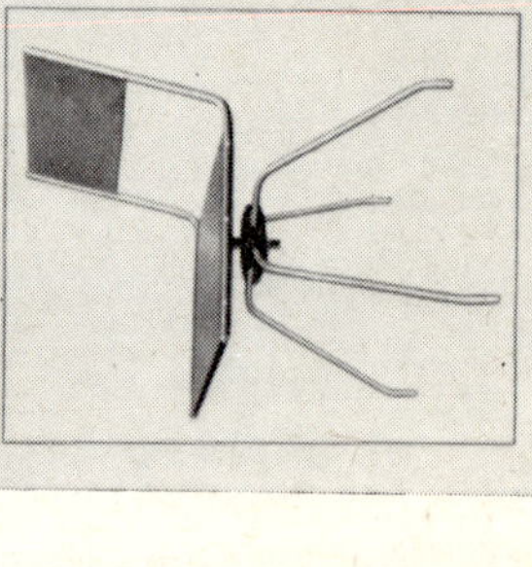

an arbitrary composition; it is a necessary component of our environment. In itself impersonal, it takes on meaning only from the way it is used or as part of a complete scheme.' [31] This preoccupation with rationalization, anonymity and standardization, is also reflected in the work of his students. Most of them worked in wood, leather and canvas, and many of the designs they produced eventually went into production.

Opposite:
Advertisement for Breuer metal furniture, made by Standard-Möbel; Marcel Breuer, 1928

Tables using tubular steel, Marcel Breuer, 1927

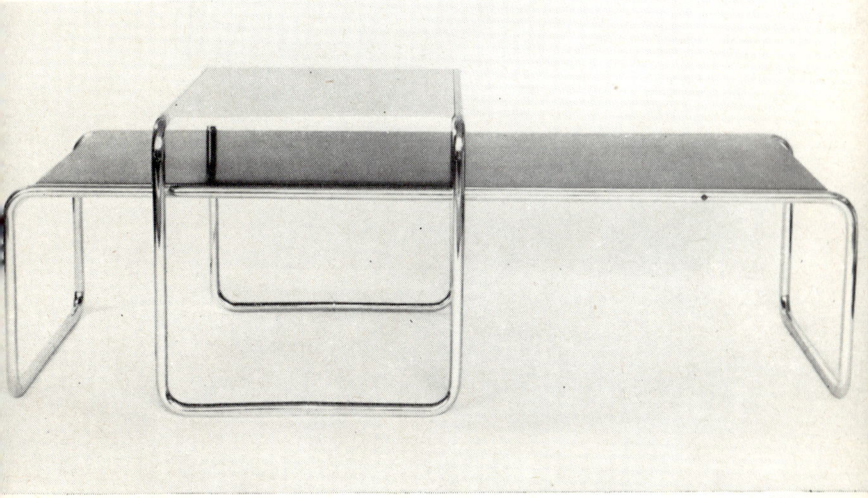

The weaving workshop soon began to enjoy a similar commercial success after the move to Dessau. In *Bauhaus Weimar-Dessau*, Anni Albers describes how the students in Weimar had 'begun amateurishly and playfully,' but as they experimented with techniques, materials, colours and textures 'a shift soon took place from free play with forms to logical composition. As a result more systematic training in the mechanics of weaving was introduced, as well as a course in the dyeing of yarns. The whole range of possibilities had been freely explored; concentration on a definite purpose now had a disciplinary effect.

'The physical quality of materials became a subject of interest. Light-reflecting and sound-absorbing materials were developed. The desire to reach a larger group of consumers brought about a transition from hand work to machine work; work by hand was for the laboratory only; work by machine was for mass production.'

Whether to concentrate on machine or hand production was a subject of some controversy in the weaving workshop, which was the only one to carry over the dual system of instruction from Weimar to Dessau. Georg Muche, who had been *Formmeister* in Weimar, retained this title in Dessau and Gunta Stölzl became his 'technical' assistant. Wingler describes how Muche's efforts to step up machine production met with some opposition from Gunta Stölzl and the students, and he reprints an article in which she claims that machine techniques were not flexible enough at that time to exploit the revolutionary advances that had been achieved in the workshops by hand-weaving methods. It was essential, she maintained, if any progress was to be made, that the hand-weaver should be given freedom to experiment, and that concentration on effects that could be achieved by contemporary machine techniques could be stultifying and inhibiting. And in any case, she concludes somewhat waspishly 'weaving is women's work'.

Wall hanging, Anni Albers, 1927

Because of this closing of ranks against him, and because he wanted to concentrate on architecture and painting, Muche relinquished his position in the workshop early in 1926, and Gunta Stölzl took sole charge. Under her leadership the weaving department did become, in fact, a 'laboratory' where new ideas were tried and tested and many of them were eventually adopted by industry. For, despite her insistence on the need for freedom to experiment and to carry out basic research, hers was an essentially practical approach, and many of the designs that she and her talented students (including Otti Berger, Anni Albers and Lis Beyer) produced, were in fact taken up by German manufacturers, who collaborated with the Bauhaus weavers in order to develop techniques to put many of these experimental designs into production.

Opposite:
Rug, Otti Berger, *c.* 1927

Fabric, Otti Berger, *c.* 1925 *Photograph courtesy Faber and Faber*

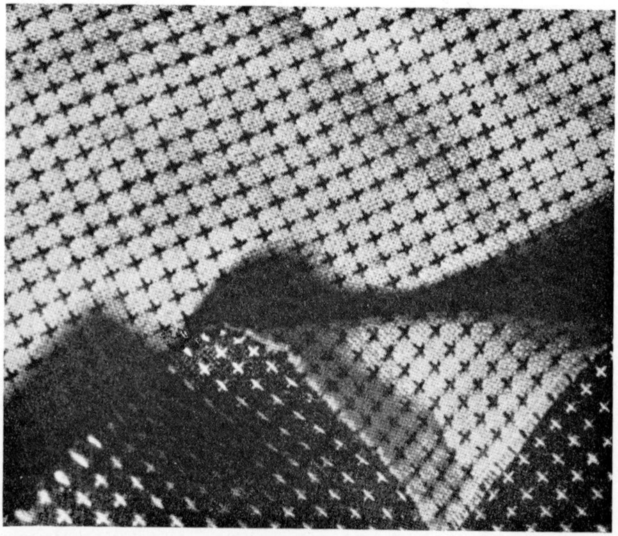

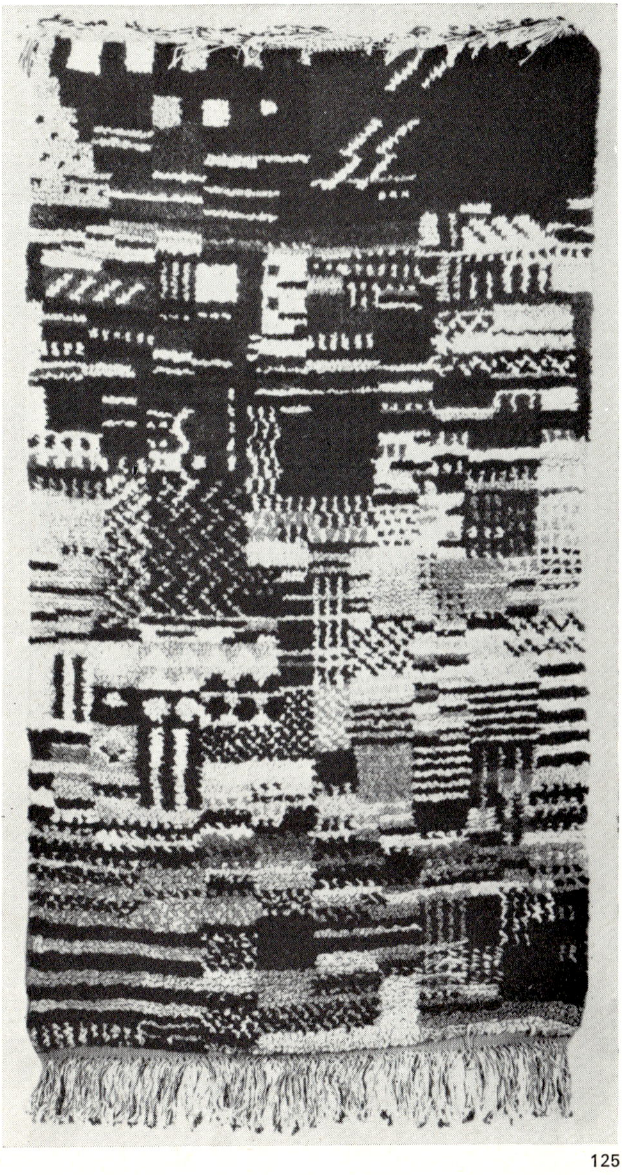

Bauhaus advertisement for a punch cutter

Opposite:
Wall hanging, triple weave, black-white-yellow silk, Anni Albers, 1926

The aims of the typography workshop were defined by Moholy-Nagy in 1923, when he wrote 'Typography must be clear communication in its most vivid form. Clarity must be especialy stressed, for clarity is the essence of modern printing. Therefore, first of all: *absolute clarity* in all typographical work. Communication ought not to labour under preconceived aesthetic notions. Letters should never be squeezed into an arbitrary shape . . . like a square. A new typographic language must be created combining elasticity, variety and a fresh approach to the materials of printing, a language whose logic depends on the appropriate application of the processes of printing.'

1928

2. jahrgang nr. 4
einzelheft preis rmk. 1.20

inhalt

die bauhausbücher

verlag albert langen, münchen, hubertusstr. 27
schriftleitung: w. gropius und l. moholy-nagy

band 1 **walter gropius, internationale architektur** (zweite auflage) geh. **5** in leinen geb. **7** rmk.
band 2 **paul klee, pädagogisches skizzenbuch** vergriffen
band 3 **ein versuchshaus des bauhauses** vergriffen
band 4 **die bühne des bauhauses** geh. **5**, in leinen geb. **7** rmk.
band 5 **piet mondrian, neue gestaltung** vergriffen
band 6 **theo van doesburg, grundbegriffe der neuen gestaltenden kunst** vergriffen
band 7 **neue arbeiten der bauhauswerkstätten** geh. **6**, in leinen geb. **8** rmk.
band 8 **l. moholy-nagy, malerei, photographie, film** (zweite auflage) geh. **7**, in leinen geb. **9** rmk.
band 9 **w. kandinsky, punkt und linie zur fläche** (zweite auflage) geh. **15**, in leinen geb. **18** rmk.
band 10 **j. j. p. oud, holländische architektur** geh. **6**, in leinen geb. **8** rmk.

neu erschienen ist:

band 11 **k. malewitsch, die gegenstandslose welt,** begründung und erklärung des russischen suprematismus geh. **6**, in leinen geb. **8** rmk.

in kürze erscheinen:

band 12 **w. gropius, bauhausneubauten in dessau**
band 13 **a. gleizes, kubismus**
band 14 **l. moholy-nagy, von kunst zu leben**

die sammlung wird fortgesetzt

die bauhaus-zeitschrift erscheint vierteljährlich

bezugspreis jährlich rmk. 4.—
einzelnummer rmk. 1.20
preis dieser nummer rmk. 1.20

abonnements bei dem verlag oder durch den buchhandel

verlag und anzeigenverwaltung: dessau, zerbster str. 16 postscheckkonto: magdeburg 16662
telefon sammel-nr. 3106
für den anzeigenteil verantwortlich: hermann steffen, dessau.

bezugs- und zahlungsbedingungen:

abonnements haben geltung bis ende des laufenden kalenderjahres. abonnements, die 30 tage vor ablauf des laufenden kalenderjahres beim verlage schriftlich nicht gekündigt sind, gelten als um das nächste kalenderjahr verlängert., erteilte rechnungen sind so zeitig zu begleichen, daß der verlag spätestens 8 tage nach rechnungsdatum über die rechnungsbeträge verfügen kann. überfällige forderungen erhöhen sich um mahn- und inkassospesen. ausfall der zeitschriftenlieferung ohne verschulden des verlages (streik, höhere gewalt usw.) berechtigt nicht zum verlangen nach minderung des bezugspreises oder schadenersatzleistung. erfüllungsort und gerichtsstand für beide teile ist dessau.

sendungen an die redaktion: bauhaus dessau

für die redaktion verantwortlich: ernst kállai, dessau.
für unverlangte beiträge und rezensionsexemplare keinerlei gewähr.

nr. 2/3 1928 der bauhauszeitschrift ist vollständig vergriffen!

Bauhaus magazine contents page, 1928

Bauhaus advertisement for building work

Moholy began to apply these ideas as soon as he joined the Bauhaus. Before 1923 the print workshop had been under the direction of Lyonel Feininger, who had concentrated mainly on the production of a series of Bauhaus albums—lithographs, woodcuts and engravings illustrating the work of contemporary artists. At that time there was no official typographer on the staff and the 'printed emphemera' of the Bauhaus showed strong Expressionist and Dada influences—leaflets, programmes, book jackets, etc., displaying a riot of symbols and letter forms, flung

Cover for the Bauhaus magazine, 1928

Cover for the Bauhaus magazine, 1929

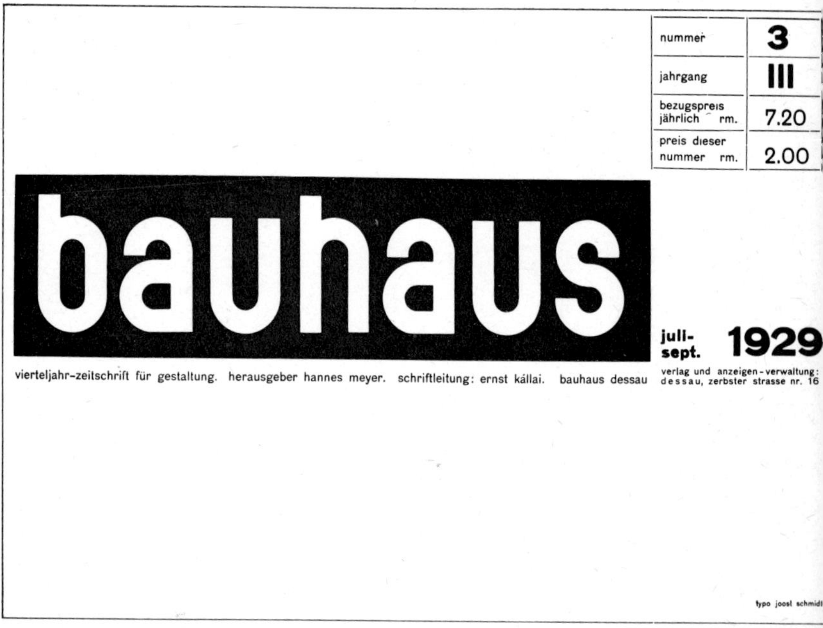

Cover, by Joost Schmidt, for the Bauhaus magazine, 1929

Opposite:
Advertisement for a printing firm, Herbert Bayer

together in anarchistic abandon. Moholy-Nagy, with his Constructivist ideals, put an end to all that, and the publicity material produced for the Bauhaus exhibition of 1923 was purged of the move exuberant typographical tricks. Josef Albers, Joost Schmidt and Herbert Bayer, who was then a student in the wall-painting workshop, began, with the encouragement of Moholy, to concentrate on graphic design, establishing the disciplines that are now taken for granted by designers in this field.

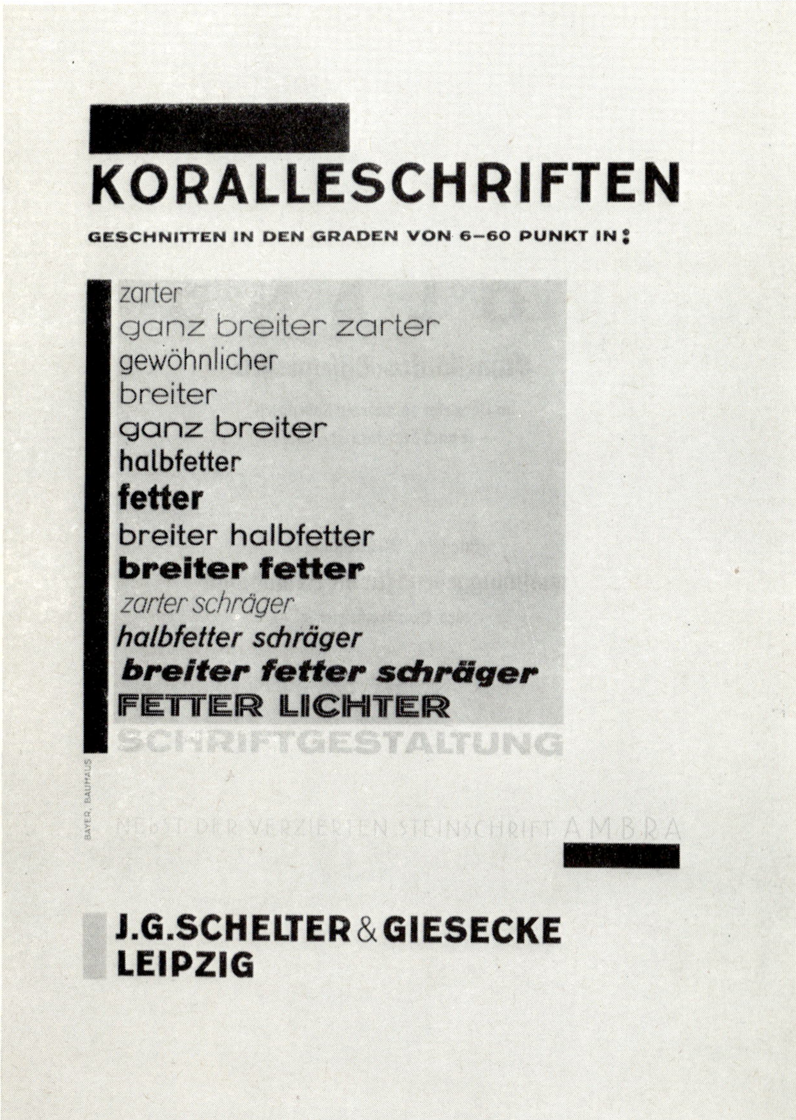
KORALLESCHRIFTEN
GESCHNITTEN IN DEN GRADEN VON 6–60 PUNKT IN:
zarter
ganz breiter zarter
gewöhnlicher
breiter
ganz breiter
halbfetter
fetter
breiter halbfetter
breiter fetter
zarter schräger
halbfetter schräger
breiter fetter schräger
FETTER LICHTER
SCHRIFTGESTALTUNG
NEBST DER VERZIERTEN STEINSCHRIFT AMBRA
BAYER, BAUHAUS
J.G.SCHELTER & GIESECKE
LEIPZIG

Pantomime, 'Treppenwitz', Oskar Schlemmer, 1925–9

Opposite:
Three figures with furniture-like forms, Oskar Schlemmer, 1929
Photograph courtesy Busch-Reisinger Museum

The Dessau Törten-Siedlung, 1928 *Photograph courtesy Faber and Faber*

'universal type', Herbert Bayer, 1925

In Dessau the typography workshop was run by Herbert Bayer, although work for the department was carried out by Moholy-Nagy, Schlemmer, Albers and Schmidt. It was after the move to Dessau that Bauhaus layouts achieved their characteristic sense of order, symmetry and clarity; information was organized and presented in carefully balanced grids; decorative elements were reduced to the basic geometric forms—circle, square and thick horizontal or vertical rule; the relationship between text and illustrations was calculated with mathematical precision and the serif was banished—a revolutionary move in Germany, where the elaborate Gothic alphabet was still widely used. In their search for clarity and legibility, Bayer and Albers both designed sans-serif typefaces, Albers' 'stencil letters' being composed of three basic shapes. Bayer also made heroic efforts to abolish the use of capital letters, on the grounds of logic, clarity and economy. 'Why should we write and print with two alphabets,' wrote Bayer, 'we do not speak with a capital A and a small a'; so, from 1925 onwards, the Bauhaus typographers began to abandon the use of upper-case letters.

der direktor

hochschule für gestaltung

postanschrift: bauhaus dessau

fernruf: 1431, 1587

bankkonto: städt. kreissparк. dessau 2634
postscheck: magdeburg 137C1

ihre zeichen | ihre nachricht vom | unsere zeichen | tag

wir schreiben alles klein, denn wir sparen damit zeit

bauhausdruck 5000

Bauhaus letterhead, Herbert Bayer, 1927

The typography department was mainly involved in work for the Bauhaus itself—publicity material, prospectuses, pamphlets, posters, etc., although it did carry out commissions for other organizations. It was not, however, directly concerned with the school's most important venture in publishing—the publication, between 1925 and 1931, of fourteen Bauhaus books. These were part of a vast series, edited by Gropius and Moholy-Nagy, in which Bauhaus staff and other leading architects and artists explained and illustrated their theories. Several of the books were designed and laid out by Moholy-Nagy; they were printed by the Verlag Albert Langer in Munich, and form what is possibly the most stimulating series in modern art to be published in this century. Fifty were planned and fourteen were published, including Klee's *Pädagogische Skizzenbuch*, a selection of the lectures he had given at Weimar between 1921 and 1922, *Malerei, Photographie und Film*, and *Von Material zu Architektur* by Moholy-Nagy, Kandinsky's *Punkt and Linie zu Fläche* and Malevich's *Die Gegenstandlose Welt*. Books by Gropius, Oud, Van Doesburg, Schlemmer and Mondrian were also included, and the series aimed to provide a complete synthesis of contemporary aesthetic thought and achievement.

Gropius's own book *Internationale Architektur*, a survey of modern European architecture, was published in 1925, two years before an independent architectural department was finally established within the Bauhaus. Gropius's decision to postpone 'official' architectural training was part conviction ('Only the journeyman who has been seasoned by workshop practice and instruction in the study of form is ready to collaborate in building,' he had written in *Idee und Aufbau*) and part necessity, since, even under the more liberal Dessau administration the Bauhaus continued to be short of the capital necessary for full-scale expansion.

Bauhaus members had, nevertheless, been involved in architectural work since 1919; the Haus am Horn, for example, was part of a scheme for a colony of houses that was to have been built from standardized components; Georg Muche and Marcel Breuer had continued in various projects to explore the problem of unit construction, and practical experience was, of course, intensified in Dessau, where staff and students were all encouraged to collaborate on designing and equipping the Bauhaus

Cover design for *Von Material zu Architektur*, L. Moholy-Nagy

Labour Exchange, Dessau, 1929: exterior and interior views *Photographs courtesy Faber and Faber*

buildings, as well as the labour exchange and housing colony that the town council had commissioned from Gropius. Early in 1927, however, soon after the Bauhaus buildings had been completed, Gropius decided to 'widen the scope of architectural training'. According to *Bauhaus Weimar Dessau*, 'specialists in Construction, Statics and Descriptive geometry were appointed to the staff', and Hannes Meyer, a Swiss architect, was asked to take charge of the architectural department. In appointing Hannes

Meyer, Gropius brought in a tough and uncompromizing realist, who was preoccupied by social and scientific rather than aesthetic problems. His was essentially a functional and rational approach and he based his architectural course on a systematic analysis of all the practical problems involved in designing a human environment. He had little affinity with the artists on the Bauhaus staff and felt that their theories and experience were scarcely relevant to the problems of design and architecture which were first and foremost social. The architect, he maintained, must be backed by the scientist, the sociologist and the psychologist if his work was to have any social meaning.

Obviously Gropius intended, with the establishment of the architectural department, to strengthen the Bauhaus's social commitments, and it is significant that it was this 'outsider' that he chose to nominate as his successor when he decided to leave the Bauhaus in 1928.

Gropius's departure came as a shock to the students; Siegfried Giedion in *Work and Teamwork* describes how he had given a lecture at the Bauhaus on the day Gropius handed in his resignation, and was at a party there when the news broke: 'In the general atmosphere of crazy high spirits there was no hint that anyone knew what had happened. At midnight the band suddenly came to a halt. The most senior student went up to Gropius and said "You have made many mistakes, Gropius, but there is no one to fill your shoes. You oughtn't to leave".'

There were several reasons for Gropius's departure; he had given nine years to the Bauhaus, and during that time administrative work had prevented him from widening the scope of his architectural practice. Even under the more liberal Dessau administration, when the still too meagre grant was supplemented by royalties from Bauhaus products, he found it difficult to pay his staff, provide free places for impecunious students and extend the scope of the courses. Moreover, the attacks on Bauhaus ideologies had been resumed. According to Wingler, Gropius felt that the more vicious were directed at him personally, and that by leaving he would give the Bauhaus peace to extend and consolidate the achievements of the past five years.

Obviously he felt that Hannes Meyer was the right man to give the Bauhaus a new sense of direction, but Meyer was hardly a popular figure when he took over in April 1928. At the party described by Giedion, one of the students had made a speech declaring that the appointment was a catastrophe for the Bauhaus. It certainly marked the end of an era, for Breuer, Moholy-Nagy and Herbert Bayer left with Gropius, and Meyer brought in new men and new objectives.

In his first address to the students as director-designate, Meyer declared that the conflicts within the Bauhaus were symptomatic of the sickness currently afflicting humanity—man's failure to communicate with man: 'Will our work be directed inwards or outwards? Shall we turn our attention to the needs of humanity,

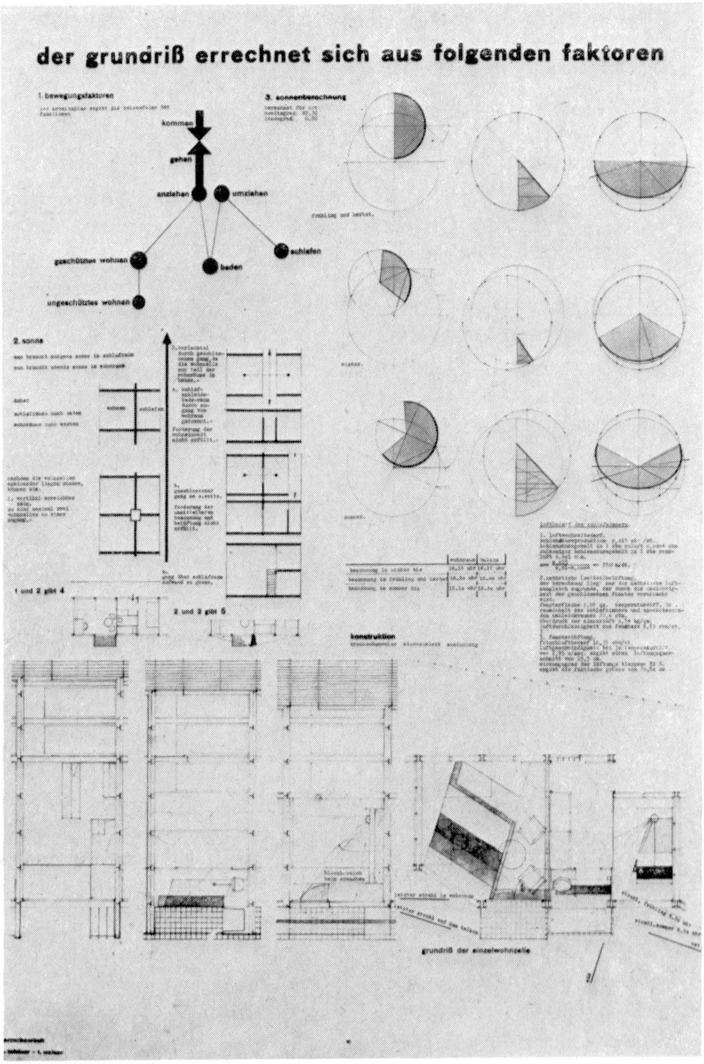

Part of a study programme for Hannes Meyer's architectural course, 1930

and collaborate in building a new way of life, or shall we become an island . . .?'[32] In order to eradicate the weaknesses he saw in the Bauhaus curriculum, Meyer extended the scope of the architectural course. He introduced studies in mathematics and engineering, and worked out a systematic course, emphasizing the architect's social responsibilities. 'Architecture,' he maintained, 'is not the individual emotional activity of an artist. Building is a collective activity' and he worked out a course that reflected his conviction that 'Building depends on organization: social, technical, economic and psychical organization'.[33] He appointed several new members of staff, including the architect and town planner Ludwig Hilberseimer, and Alfred Arndt, who had studied at the Bauhaus from 1921–6. Walter Peterhans took charge of a special course in photography and Mart Stam was appointed guest lecturer. During the two years of Meyer's directorship the Bauhaus architectural department was involved in extending the Dessau Törten-Siedlung, the housing estate that Gropius had designed in the outskirts of Dessau, and the students also collaborated in the design of a Trades Union school in Bernau, near Berlin, which was completed in 1930. Also under Meyer's régime, the workshops stepped up production, and more and more Bauhaus designs were mass produced, so that the school's income from royalties was practically doubled.

But in spite of his obvious competence and his success as a teacher, Meyer's extreme left-wing views soon brought him into conflict with the Dessau authorities. He encouraged the students to participate in political activities and this was of course anathema in the Germany of 1930. Meyer, however, refused to compromise; for him, building was first and foremost a social activity and he believed that no true architect could remain politically uncommitted. In the summer of 1930, he was asked to resign, and he published a bitter letter in a Berlin journal revealing his complete contempt for the values he found in the Bauhaus when he took over the school. Hours were spent, he declared, designing teacups according to Constructivist principles, and a vague medieval inspired socialism permeated the school. 'This was the basis of my tragi-comic situation; as director of the Bauhaus I found myself fighting the Bauhaus style . . . I taught the students to relate building to the community; I weaned them from the formalistic,

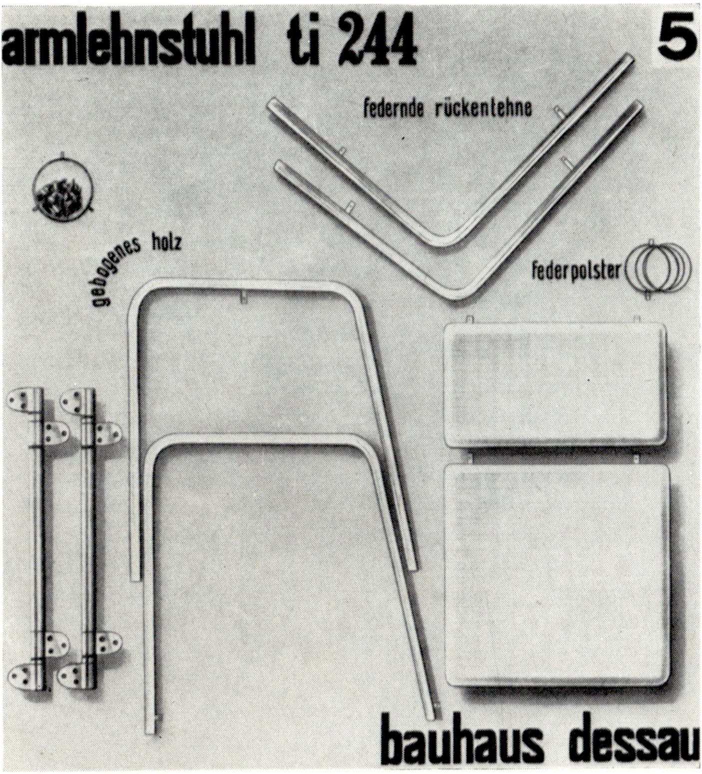

Demountable armchair, Josef Albers, 1929

intuitive approach and taught them to undertake basic research; I showed them how to put the needs of the people first.'[34]

Although these were extravagant claims, Meyer's short régime did have positive results. He laid the foundation for a practical and systematic course in architecture; he increased the students' social awareness and he strengthened the school's ties with industry. But his intolerance and his fanaticism were inherently stultifying: there was no room for anyone whose opinions differed from his own, and the liberal, essentially humanistic attitudes that Gropius had encouraged were rejected. Conflicting factors within the Bauhaus were again threatening to destroy it and a more impartial and objective leader had to be found.

When Meyer left, the Dessau administration tried to persuade Gropius to take over again, but he refused, and he suggested that the architect Mies van der Rohe should be offered the directorship.

Gropius had first met Mies van der Rohe in Behrens' office before the First World War; after the war Mies, like Gropius, had become involved in the activities of the Novembergruppe, and until 1927 his growing reputation as an architect was based on various projects he designed for the group's exhibitions—the glass skyscrapers of 1919 and 1920, the office building in reinforced concrete of 1921 and the villas of 1923 and 1924. In 1927, Mies took charge of the Deutscher Werkbund's Weissenhof-Siedlung exhibition in Stuttgart, for which he, Gropius, Le Corbusier, Behrens and many other leading architects designed houses and apartment blocks, and in 1928 he confirmed his international reputation with his design for the German pavilion at Barcelona.

Project for a glass skyscraper, Mies van der Rohe, 1920–1

Barcelona Pavilion, Mies van der Rohe, 1929

Barcelona Pavilion

He brought to the Bauhaus his reputation as a purist and a perfectionist, with a passion for order, clarity and quality. One of his first moves as director was to banish politics from his school, which made him very unpopular, for a time, with the students. Gradually, however, they began to respect his objectivity and his insistence on the highest possible standards. Under Mies's direction the architectural studies at the Bauhaus were intensified, and for a time it seemed as though the school had gained a new lease of life. But Mies was faced with a far grimmer political situation than Gropius had ever had to contend with. In August 1932, the Nazi party had gained control of the province of Anhalt, which included Dessau, and its officials immediately took steps to close the Bauhaus—for them a symbol of Bolshevism, decadence and subversion. Mies and Dr Fritz Hesse tried to persuade them to reverse the decision, which had aroused a storm of international protest, but the school's fanatical opponents were not prepared to listen to reason, and the Dessau Bauhaus was closed in October 1932.

Mies, however, managed to re-open the school as a private venture in Berlin; he rented an empty telephone factory and the Bauhaus re-established itself there for six uneasy months. Then Hitler came into power and the persecution was resumed. On

Barcelona chair, Mies van der Rohe, 1929

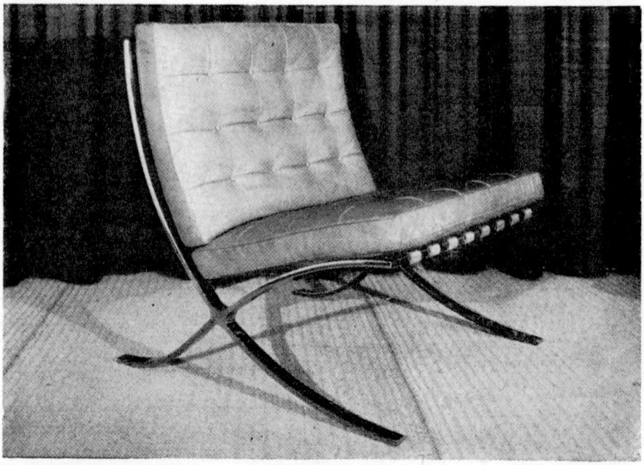

11 April 1933 the Gestapo occupied the school, searched it for evidence of Communist activities, and forbade the students and staff re-entry. For several weeks Mies attempted to persuade the new régime to re-open the school, but he could not accept the conditions that were imposed, and the school was finally closed down in July 1933.

Then the exodus began; Klee went to Switzerland and Kandinsky to Paris, but most of the staff eventually found teaching posts in the States: Gropius, after spending three years in England, was appointed head of Harvard School of Architecture; this was in 1937, and later that same year, Marcel Breuer joined him, and they set up an architectural practice. Mies van der Rohe stayed in Germany until 1937, when he was asked to teach at the Illinois Institute of Technology (then known as the Armour Institute); Hilberseimer, Peterhans and several of the students joined him there. Moholy-Nagy founded a New Bauhaus (later renamed Institute of Design) in Chicago; Albers was appointed professor of art at the Black Mountain College, North Carolina; Bayer became art director of an advertising agency in New York, so that Bauhaus ideals and teaching methods began to be adopted and adapted by art and architectural schools throughout the world.

Chair, Marcel Breuer, 1936

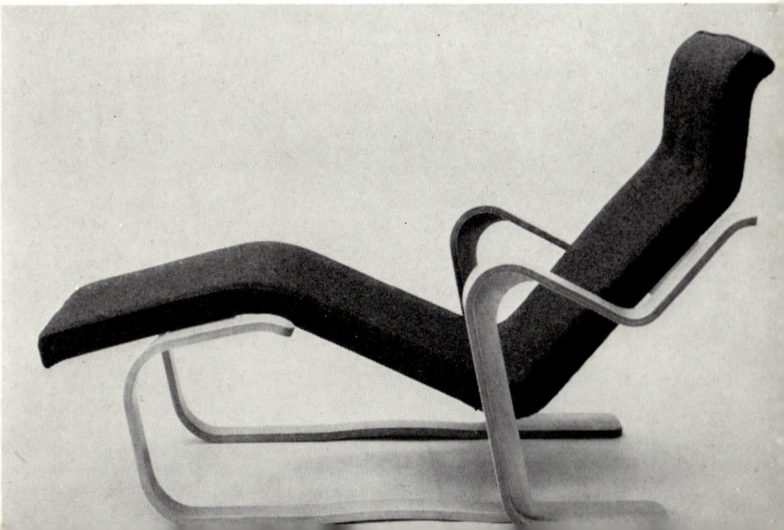

Conclusion

'When I was a boy my family was living in a city apartment with open gas-jets, individual coal-heated stoves in each room, including the bathroom, where the warm water was heated for the bath each Saturday: that took two hours. There was no electric street car, no automobile, of course, no plane.

'Radio, film, gramophone, X-ray, telephone were non-existent.'[35]

This was the society that Gropius grew up in; even in 1919, when the Bauhaus was founded, the world still seemed comparatively simple, and the idea of planning for environmental reform not entirely Utopian. But during the next twenty years technology made its take-over bid, and no reformers, no matter how well organized or well intentioned, could keep pace with the change.

Although frustrated by political and economic revolutions, the Bauhaus made the bravest and the most practical attempt; but as Gropius was to point out, it could not move faster than the society that it sought to serve. The school was essentially a product of the 'twenties, and although the Bauhaus idea of co-operative effort to promote creative work has influenced design and architectural training throughout the world, the school's practical achievements must be judged in the context of the inter-war years.

Gropius, who combined nineteenth-century idealism with twentieth-century realism, was convinced that the key to reform lay in education, but his ideas on what should be taught and how it should be taught, gradually matured as the Bauhaus adapted itself to meet sociological change. In Weimar, Gropius believed that painters could be taught techniques to civilize industry. 'Modern painting,' he wrote in 1923, 'breaking through old conventions, has released countless suggestions which are still waiting to be used by the practical world. But when, in the future, artists who sense new creative values have practical training in the industrial world, they will themselves possess the means for realising those values immediately. They will compel industry to serve their ideas and industry will seek out and use their comprehensive training.'[36]

In earlier cultures links between art and product design were forged more or less unconsciously, and the idea that the artist could be taught the skills to establish formulae that would unite all the arts, including architecture and design, was originated by the nineteenth-century reformers, and revived in the first twenty years of the twentieth century by Futurist and Constructivist polemics. The Weimar Bauhaus was the first full-scale attempt to put these theories into practice, and it soon became obvious that the ideals of the artist and those of industry were irreconcilable, and that entirely new disciplines were required to bridge the gap between art and technology.

In establishing these disciplines the Bauhaus evolved a teaching programme that was radical and revolutionary; as the programme developed, its emphasis shifted from 'art' and 'craftsmanship' to 'technique' (in its broadest sense, which acknowledges social demands). Moholy-Nagy was the last painter to join the staff, and he was appointed in 1923; in Dessau the dual system of instruction was abandoned and as the workshops became more productive the Bauhaus artist became more and more of a background figure, until in Meyer's and Mies's era, he was more or less redundant.

Nevertheless, the fact that Klee and Kandinsky remained at the Bauhaus until its last years (Klee left at the end of 1929 and Kandinsky moved to Berlin with Mies), is a tribute to the flexibility of the school's educational programme and to the tenacity of Gropius's belief in the 'common citizenship of all forms of creative work'.

Fine art values, of course, contributed a great deal to the emergence, after 1923, of a recognizable Bauhaus style—a style based on the cube, the rectangle and the circle, which reflected the preoccupations of the Constructivists and the Cubists and which, after some trial and error, lent itself to contemporary production techniques; but by the time the Bauhaus had established strong links with industry, in spite of Hannes Meyer's criticisms, the original impetus for the style had been abandoned, social preoccupations were ousting fine art values and the quest for the immutable 'type-form' was replaced by research into the rationalization and humanization of mass produced goods.

The Bauhaus has been criticized for not being more radical in its approach to product design, for looking, as Buckminster-Fuller puts it, 'at problems of modification of the surface of end products, which end products were inherently sub-functions of a technically obsolete world'.

This is a fundamental dilemma, and it still faces architects and designers and those responsible for their training today. No matter how rapidly man adjusts to technological change, he cannot keep pace with all the social, economic, psychological and political implications of technology.

In the Bauhaus Gropius taught that the designer's first responsibility is to his client; that he cannot attempt to impose new patterns of life based on revolutionary design solutions before society is ready to accept them. 'Not the product, but man, is the end in view,' wrote Moholy-Nagy when he came to describe the Bauhaus's achievements.[37] It is this essential humanism, based on an attempt to understand man's psychological as well as his physical needs, that has been the Bauhaus's most important contribution to twentieth-century architecture and design. 'The wholeness of its approach,' wrote Gropius, 'has helped to restore the architecture and design of today as a social art.'[38]

But this wholeness depended on the collaboration and mutual sympathy of a group of specialists all working towards a common aim. 'We began over there in the Bauhaus,' wrote Klee. 'We began there with a community to which each of us gave what he had.

'More we cannot do.'[39]

List of Sources

1 **The Scope of Total Architecture,** Walter Gropius, Harper and Row, New York 1953; Allen & Unwin, London, 1956
2 **New Architecture and the Bauhaus,** Walter Gropius, M.I.T. Press, Cambridge, Mass.; Faber and Faber, London, 1935
3 *Ibid.*
4 **Bauhaus Weimar 1919–25 Dessau 1925–28,** Charles T. Branford, Boston, 1952
5 **New Architecture and the Bauhaus** *op. cit.*
6 **Seven Lamps of Architecture,** John Ruskin, 1848
7 'The Lesser Arts', 1878, lecture by William Morris
8 Article in **Commonweal,** 1885
9 **Dekorative Kunst,** Munich, 1898; quoted from *Art Nouveau,* R. Schmutzler, Thames and Hudson, 1964
10 **Walter Gropius, Work and Teamwork,** Siegfried Giedion, Architectural Press, 1954
11 **Die Renaissance im modernen Kunstgewerbe,** 1903; quoted from 'Pioneers of Modern Design', N. Pevsner, Penguin Books, 1960
12 **Das Bauhaus,** Hans Wingler, Verlag Gebr. Rasch & Co, Osnabruck, 1963; extracts quoted from this work have been translated by Gillian Naylor
13 **Bauhaus Weimar—Dessau** *op. cit.*
14 **Bauhaus Weimar—Dessau** *op. cit.*
15 *Ibid.*
16 **Crafts of the Weimar Bauhaus,** Walther Scheidig, Edition Leipzig, 1966; Studio Vista, London, 1967
17 **Das Bauhaus** *op. cit.*
18 **Bauhaus Weimar—Dessau** *op. cit.*
19 **Architectural Review,** August 1957
20 *Ibid.*
21 **De Stijl,** H. L. C. Jaffé, Amsterdam 1956
22 *Ibid.*
23 *Ibid.*
24 **The New Vision and Abstract of an Artist,** L. Moholy-Nagy, New York (revised edition), 1947
25 **Das Bauhaus** *op. cit.*
26 **The New Architecture and the Bauhaus** *op. cit.*
27 *Ibid.*
28 **The New Vision and Abstract of an Artist** *op. cit.*
29 **Form 37,** Westdeutschen Verlag [German design quarterly]
30 **Bauhaus Weimar—Dessau** *op. cit.*
31 *Ibid.*
32 **Das Bauhaus** *op. cit.*
33 *Ibid.*
34 *Ibid.*
35 **Design and Industry,** Walter Gropius, 1950
36 **Idee und Aufbau des Staatlichen Bauhauses Weimar**
37 **The New Vision and Abstract of an Artist** *op. cit.*
38 **The Scope of Total Architecture** *op. cit.*
39 **On Modern Art,** lecture given by Paul Klee, Jena 1924; Faber and Faber, London 1966

The author and publishers are grateful to Raschverlag, Osnabrück and M.I.T. Press, Cambridge, Mass. for permission to reproduce from *Das Bauhaus* by Hans Maria Wingler the illustrations on the following pages: 27, 58, 68, 86, 96, 97, 104, 113, 118 (top), 120, 125, 126, 134, 139, 141, 145, 147

Index

(Numbers in italics refer to illustrations)